The
Best of
Davie
Napier

The
Best of
Davie
Napier

❏ Come Sweet Death
❏ Time of Burning
❏ Word of God,
  Word of Earth

Davie
Napier

ABINGDON PRESS

Nashville

Library of Congress Cataloging-in-Publication Data

Napier, Bunyan Davie.
    The best of Davie Napier / B. Davie Napier.
        p.   cm.
    Includes bibliographical references.
    Contents: Come sweet death—Time of burning—Word of God, word of earth.
    ISBN 0-687-02827-2 (acid-free paper)
    1. Bible. O.T. Genesis—Meditations. 2. Bible. O.T.—Paraphrases, English. 3. Bible. O.T.—Meditations. 4. Elijah (Biblical character) 5. Bible. O.T. Kings, 1st, XVII-XIX, XXI—Criticism, interpretation, etc. 6. Pastoral theology. I. Napier, Bunyan Davie. Come sweet death. 1992. II. Napier, Bunyan Davie. Time of burning. 1992. III. Napier, Bunyan Davie. Word of God, word of earth. 1992. IV. Title.
BS1235.4.N29   1992
221.6—dc20   92-22864

Scripture quotations, unless otherwise noted, are from the New Revised Standard Version of the Bible, copyright 1989 by the Division of Christian Education of the National Council of the Churches of Christ in the USA. Used by permission.

In instances where the New Revised Standard Version uses *the LORD*, the author has substituted the word *Yahweh.*

Those noted RSV are from the Revised Standard Version of the Bible, copyright © 1946, 1952, 1971 by the Division of Christian Education of the National Council of the Churches of Christ in the USA. Used by permission.

Those noted REB are from The Revised English Bible. Copyright © Oxford University Press and Cambridge University Press. Used by permission.

Those noted KJV are from the King James Version of the Bible.

Those noted NJB are from The New Jerusalem Bible, copyright © 1985 by Darton, Longman & Todd, and Doubleday & Company, Inc. Reprinted by permission of the publishers.

The quotation on pp. 165-66 is from "How to Begin a Glorious Day," excerpted from Guideposts Magazine. Copyright © 1974 by Guideposts Associates, Inc., Carmel, N. Y. 10512.

DEDICATION

To Joy, for fifty-plus years as spouse, companion, critic, editor, disturber-of-my-peace, my only barber (since 1967), vigorous deflator/inflator (as indicated) of my ego, lifelong lover and friend;

To those who have listened and responded to my preaching in all conceivable settings, to my teaching in seminar and classroom at Judson, Alfred, Georgia (U of), Yale, Stanford, Pacific School of Religion, and Mount Holyoke, and to my published writings (reading can be listening) in articles and books and symposia since 1940;

To those who wittingly or not have instructed me, humiliated me, set me on course again (or off course), taught me to see and to hear what might have passed me by unheeded, and who have left part of their life in me;

To Betty Lile of Little Rock, who for decades has singularly encouraged me in my writing and my work;

To all of the above, to scores of other folk living and dead who have touched me beneficently; and above all to Yahweh-of-the-Prophets, Christ-of-the-Apostles, and Spirit-of-the-Disciples, I fervently and gratefully dedicate these lines out of my past and present, here revived, reappropriated, recast, renewed, reconceived, redirected, and recommitted.

CONTENTS

PREFACE

Here are excerpts from the introductions to the First and Revised editions of *Come Sweet Death:*

> While some of the stories in the early chapters of Genesis are no doubt drawn from myths of the ancient Near East, it is clear that the stories have undergone a theological refinement in the mouths and hands of [ancient] Israel's tellers and recorders. . . . But in one regard, they retain the myth quality: the stories exist, they are told and retold, recorded and read and reread, not for their *wasness* but for their *isness.*

From the Revised Edition:

> The title phrase "Come, sweet death" is first formed in these verse-essays as a bitter human protest: If this is what creation is, then you can take it, Yahweh. But as the textual settings move from Garden to Brothers to Flood to Tower to Land, that title phrase becomes a succinct prayer of petition and gratitude for Jesus Christ—Come, Sweet Death!
>
> [What is depicted is] the essential, perennial human condition of destructive pride which begins to be biblically answered in the story of the Land—the purpose of God to bless the families of the earth.

And from the introduction to the original *Time of Burning:*

> Every generation continues to read with immediate meaning the varied stuff of biblical literature because it never simply "was" but always "is."

This is a quartet from the Prophets, a free, present-tense reading of narratives about three real [prophets] and one just as real but not historical, not in the realm of facticity—Moses, Isaiah, Jeremiah, and Jonah. These readings are free and contemporary in the sense that I have taken the liberty of putting us into them.

And from the first *Word of God, Word of Earth:*

My own preparation . . . began with a fresh, critical reading and translation of the Hebrew texts of I Kings 17–19:21, and I have reproduced, as preface to each of the chapters, the results of my work as editor and translator. . . . Such dramatic stories as these have inevitably drawn additions, accretions, from subsequent traditionalists. These edited translations are simply one modern reader's effort, in consultation with the works of scholars of this century, to achieve a reading more closely approximating what may well have been the Elijah material as it took form in the years during and immediately following his own time.

Here we are making our move into a new century, and I am gathering (some of) my best from the old in an effort to shape it to the new, or more immediately to this present time between centuries, so to speak. True revision, renewal (see my Dedication) really requires reappropriation. It doesn't come about painlessly. At one point early in that work, I scratched this line to my editor: "Have had a *terrible* time with revisions of older writing, but begin to think it may be viable. . . . I still hope we can pull something off!"

In any case, here it is, out of a process which has proved to be for me sometimes discouraging and frustrating, but in the end always gratifying and even exciting. I hope the reading of it may be so for you, the readers, who may have read me before, or even seen and heard me in your *Disciple* circles.

Finally, we can all be grateful to the Holy Spirit, and to the faithful hands and minds that gave us this Treasure, this Sacred Scripture, this Bible.

PART ONE

Come Sweet Death

CHAPTER ONE

The Garden

Genesis 2–3

2:7 Then Yahweh God formed man from the dust of the ground, and breathed into his nostrils the breath of life; and the man became a living being.

2:8-9 And Yahweh God planted a garden in Eden, in the east; and there he put the man whom he had formed. Out of the ground Yahweh God made to grow every tree that is pleasant to the sight and good for food, the tree of life also in the midst of the garden, and the tree of the knowledge of good and evil.

2:15-17 Yahweh God took the man and put him in the garden of Eden to till it and keep it. And Yahweh God commanded the man, "You may freely eat of every tree of the garden; but of the tree of the knowledge of good and evil you shall not eat, for in the day that you eat of it you shall die."

2:20 The man gave names to all cattle, and to the birds of the air, and to every animal of the field; but for the man there was not found a helper as his partner.

2:22, 25 Yahweh God . . . made . . . a woman and brought her to the man. . . . And the man and his wife were both naked, and were not ashamed.

3:1-13 Now the serpent . . . said to the woman, "Did God say, 'You shall not eat from any tree in the garden'?" The woman said to the serpent, "We may eat of the fruit of the trees in the garden; but God said, 'You shall not eat of the fruit of the tree that is in the middle of the garden, nor shall you touch it, or you shall die.'" But the serpent said to the woman, "You will not die. For God knows that when you eat of it your eyes will be opened, and you will be like God, knowing good and evil." So when the woman saw that the tree was good for food, and that it was a delight to the eyes, and that the tree was to be desired to make one wise, she took of its fruit and ate; and she also gave some to her husband . . . and he ate. Then the eyes of both were opened, and they knew that they were naked. . . . They heard the sound of Yahweh God walking in the garden at the time of the evening breeze, and the man and his wife hid themselves from the presence of Yahweh God among the trees of the garden. But Yahweh God called to the man, and said to him, "Where are you?" He said, "I heard the sound of you in the garden, and I was afraid, because I was naked; and I hid myself." He said, "Who told you that you were naked? Have you eaten from the tree of which I commanded you not to eat?" The man said, "The woman whom you gave to be with me, she gave me fruit from the tree, and I ate." Then Yahweh God said to the woman, "What is this that you have done?" The woman said, "The serpent tricked me, and I ate."

3:16-17 [Yahweh God said] to the woman . . .
"I will greatly increase your pangs
in childbearing. . . ."

3:19 And to the man he said, ". . . cursed is the ground because of you;
in toil you shall eat of it . . . until you return to the ground, for out of it you were taken.
you are dust, and to dust you shall return."

3:23 Therefore Yahweh God sent him forth from the garden of Eden. . . .

3:24 He drove out the man. . . .

Genesis 2:7-8 *And Yahweh Elohim forms us of dust*
(paraphrased) *and breathes the breath of life into our nostrils;*
and we become a living entity.
God plants a garden in the east (it could as
well be west or south or north), and there
in Eden Yahweh Elohim ordains
that we shall be. . . .

I

This is the garden, Yahweh?
This little plot, this planet earth, this globe
assaulting me in arbitrary sequence
with wind and earthquake, fire, and still small voices;
providing me, in weary alternation,
with snow and sun and rain, seedtime and harvest;
with storm and drought and flood and hurricane
with searing desert heat and numbing cold;
inflicting on me now cacophonous din
and now the sound of thin and gentle silence;
confronting me in sick juxtaposition
with appetizing foods and pesticides,
with cooling drink and nuclear pollution?
This is the garden?

II

Where, Yahweh, am I?
If this is east, then east of what or whom?
I must be east of you, you big Direction.
   Or somewhere east of Suez
   on the road to Mandalay
   on the road to Mount Olympus
   on the road to Canterbury
   on the road to Jericho—
      With Pilgrim Folk, U.S. Marines
      Samaritans and Alexander
      Lewis and Clark and Don Quixote
      Lee and Grant, Schwarzkopf and Patton
      (Stormin' Norman, Blood & Guts),
      and Eisenhower and MacArthur
Did all of these in fact perceive The Road?

The Road! My God, I have to know The Road.
I need to go and come and go again.
Your garden is a prison—or a tomb—
without The Road.

III

2:15

You call the garden Eden?
Eden schmeeden
tillit schmillit
keepit schmeepit.
So you can take it, God—and bleep it, God.
I did not ask you, great I AM, for Eden;
I never made request for garden space.
This place all too apparently is yours;
and no one wants the owner with the space,
not even if the flat is free.

2:20

Besides,
a something indescribable is missing,
a something sweet and soft and warm responding,
a something yielding, melting, something giving,
a something that is something like a dame.
But there is simply nothing like a dame.

IV

2:16-17

You speak a pious, childish doggerel
that sings like "Mary Had a Little Lamb"
Freely eat of every tree
every tree every tree
freely eat of every tree
nothing I deny

but the tree of good and evil
good and evil good and evil
but the tree of good and evil
  eat of it and die.
Behold, God's wondrous gift is given—with strings.
All glory be to thee, uncertain Giver,
who wants to have the gift and give it too.
I know about your damned restricted tree:
it symbolizes you and your dominion.
To spare its fruit is to acknowledge you.

Now hear this, God: the Giver with the gift
is strictly for the birds and fish and beasts.
I am a Man, made in the godly image,
made to receive and rule the gift of God.
God is for giving. Give, then, and get out.

Go now, Creator, spin some other worlds.
I cut you off, I sever all your moorings.
Drift, God, irrelevant and impotent,
along uncharted seas of vacuous space.
The earth belongs to me, and all its fullness,
the world and every living creature in it;
2:20   since it was I who named each single item
in this vast, complicated, awesome structure.

Dominion given cannot be reclaimed.
By act of God, this land is "man's" dominion
from this day forth, and evermore forever.

V

2:21-25   Now here is something new under the sun.
This place, this little kingdom of a garden
may after all be tolerably fair.

O what a piece of work is woman Eve!
What hath God wrought!

What have we wrought together,
Yahweh and I, and I and God together.

What have we wrought *together?* Eve is Eve
because I thirst and hunger: Eve exists
to meet my longing, bring to peace my passion,
and all my restlessness to resolution.

So Eve is mine, flesh of my yearning flesh.
Sweet Eve is mine, mother of all creation.

VI

Eve is a fruit tree, Eve a fecund goddess.
I take from Eve the fruit that is forbidden,
3:6   fruit good for food (and for the inward fire);
delightful to the eyes (with tactile gifts);
desired to make one wise (O wisdom sweet).

You hanger-on to life and earth and time
who will alone be loved, adored, and served,
you circumscribing, circumcising Yahweh—
I eat whatever fruit I please to eat.
Right now and any now I'm taking Eve,
which is to say I take dominion here.

I'm taking Eve. I'm taking Ecstasy.
All glory be to thee, O Ecstasy,
Almighty Eve, O Verbless Conjugation,
O Secret, Sacred Wonder of the Meeting.
Hail, Holy Meeting, Mother of the earth,
and farewell, Yahweh—have a splendid day!

VII

Come, Eve, and lie with me
under the greenwood tree.
For we are good together, good and evil,
and we are warm together, smooth and warm,
and we are one together, one and one.
Under the greenwood tree no one can see,
not even God, that sexless deity.
So come and lie with me
under the greenwood tree,
the serpent, I, and thee.
We have this time, this Eve, this ecstasy:
we have this knowledge of our nakedness.
So come, sweet Eve, and come sweet ecstasy.

VIII

3:8
Good God; I think it's Yahweh
out walking in the garden
in the coolness of the day.

And looking for a waltz.
Who wants to waltz with Yahweh
in the coolness of the day?

Who wants to sing the words:
"God walks and talks with me,
Speaks tender words to me"
in the coolness of the day?

3:9
Where are you? Can't you see, all-seeing Seer?
I'm picking daisies here with Mother Eve,
daisies of good and evil, smooth and warm,
of one and one . . . she loves me, loves me not.
You have some better word on what to do?

3:11 *Who told you you were naked?* This is good.
Who told me, God? So tell me when I'm drunk;
or maybe that I ought to see the barber;
but I can manage this one by myself.
Or shall I say in abject piety,
"All humankind is naked in your sight"?

3:11 *Then have you eaten of the tree? The* tree?
My God! You plant existence in a forest,
a veritable jungle where one cannot
discern one's right hand from one's left, and then
expect me to distinguish tree from tree!
I skipped the merit badge for trees. I am
no forest ranger. Trees! Be more specific:

2:9, 17 the tree of life . . . the tree of moral knowledge
(or is it existential "good and evil"?) . . .

2:9, 3:3 the tree which grows (in Brooklyn) "in the midst"
(in Birmingham and Belsen "in the midst"
in Brisbane, Buenos Aires, and the Bronx
and "in the midst" of Bergen and Beirut,
of Bombay, Babylon, and Bethlehem—
that pregnant tree is always in the midst!)
and finally, compounding this confusion,
you say without a clarifying word,

3:11 "the tree from which I told you not to eat."

Come now, Yahweh, this is ridiculous.
You ask about a tree; almighty God,
forget your silly tree. I will "confess"—

3:12 the woman whom *you* gave to be with me,
she gave me fruit.

3:13 *What have you done?* All right.
No more than this: We take the gift with thanks
but spurn the Giver's counsel for its use;
or at the very worst, the gift accepted,
we ostracize the still-possessive Giver.

3:13 It may be said we were beguiled (a term
in any case untrue, since, if deceived,
we wished to be deceived). But we were not.
We gained the promised knowledge, and we live,
enjoying it.

You are the problem, God.
You *force* us into disobedience—
and that's a matter simply of perspective.
The theologians want to call it pride
or even by the stronger term, rebellion.
The pious make the charge apostasy
and hypocrites will cry idolatry.
But this is nonsense, God. It is our nature
(you ought to know, who mixed the hot ingredients)
to spurn the docile role of subjugation;
to be not merely creature but creator;
to stand alone; to cherish in ourselves
all requisite resources for renewal;

Isaiah 40:31   to mount with wings as eagles
to run and not be weary
to walk and not to faint.

You give us all creation, to be sure—
then shake a disembodied godly finger
in our face about a special tree.
Well, God Almighty, if you are almighty
let us be free of you—or let us die!

It is the same, you say, you stubborn God?
Then count me out, I say—and come sweet death!

IX

Genesis 3:16   *And I will greatly multiply your pain*
3:17   *in bearing children. . . . Cursed is the ground*
because of you; now eat of it in toil.

3:19   *Since dust you are, to dust you shall return.*
3:23-24   *Then Yahweh Elohim sent them away . . .*
              to till the ground from which they had been taken.

This is a fine romance. A fine romance
this is. A beautiful relationship—
the Potter and the animated clay;
Creator and the free, creative creature;
the Parent and the independent child—
a beautiful relationship is fractured
for nothing but a silly little tree.

For you, an empty, loveless, lonely garden;
for us, a life of meanness and frustration.
Congratulations, God. Good show. Well done.

X

Sweet Eve, you say you thought you heard God
    laugh?

Hosea 11:8   I heard God say, *"How can I give you up?*
How can I hand you over?" Then a word
about another silly little tree—
an antidotal tree, redemptive tree.
And then—this must be when you thought God
    laughed—
I think I heard a sob.

I think God wept.

CHAPTER TWO

The Brothers

Genesis 4

3:1-7 Now the man knew his wife Eve, and she conceived and bore Cain. . . . Next she bore his brother Abel. Now Abel was a keeper of sheep, and Cain a tiller of the ground.

And Yahweh had regard for Abel and his offering, but [none] for Cain and his offering. . . . So Cain was very angry, and his countenance fell. Yahweh said to Cain, "Why are you angry, and why has your countenance fallen? If you do well, will you not be accepted?"

3:8-9 Cain said to his brother Abel, "Let us go out to the field." And when they were in the field, Cain rose up against his brother Abel, and killed him. Then Yahweh said to Cain, "Where is your brother Abel?" He said, "I do not know; am I my brother's keeper?"

3:10-12 And Yahweh said, "What have you done? Listen; your brother's blood is crying out to me from the ground! And now you are cursed from the ground . . . it will no longer yield to you its strength; you will be a fugitive and a wanderer on the earth."

3:13-14 Cain said . . . "My punishment is greater than I can bear! Today you have driven me away from the soil, and I shall be hidden from your face; . . . and anyone who meets me may kill me."

3:15 And Yahweh put a mark on Cain, so that no one who came upon him would kill him.

Genesis 4:1-2 *Now Adam knew Eve his wife, and she conceived*
(RSV) *and bore Cain . . . again, . . . his brother Abel.*

I

One was a shepherd, one would till the ground;
one occupied the high land, one the low;
one practiced circumcision, one abhorred it;
one was contemplative, the other bold.
The one was one, the other was the other.

> One was dark and one was light
> one was brown and one was white
> one was north and one was south
> one had plenty one knew drought
> one was west and one was east
> one was layman one was priest
> one was soldier one was sailor
> one a blacksmith one a tailor
> one was dreamer one a doer
> one a caveman one a wooer.

One was one and one the other
each to each a bloody brother
one liked desert one liked rain—
one *is* Abel . . . one *is* Cain.

II

4:3-5   There's Abel over there, the fair-haired Abel,
the tight and tidy Abel—able Abel:
the ordered life, a time for everything;
existence neatly harnessed, firmly reined.
There's Abel over there, the backward Abel.
He stinks, you know, he literally stinks:
> sweats too much and bathes too little,
> fouls his streets with dung and spittle,

the great unwashed. And arrogant! He thinks
that he is God's and all the world is his.

There's Abel over there, the oddball Abel,
Abel who differs—that's all right. But, oh,
how much he cherishes the difference,
not only in himself but in his God!
This Abel has devised an oddball God.
Of course I cannot altogether blame him:
no proper God—the Only God, that is—
would enter into league with such a man.
And what a spectacle my brother makes,
the brazen nonconformist, hatching plots
I know to seize the fruits of all creation.

I hate his guts, I hate the guts of Abel.
I'm sick of Abel, sick to death of Abel.

Sick of Brother sick of Fellows
Blacks and Reds and Browns and Yellows
sick of each minority
pressing for autonomy
sick of white men ugly white men
arrogant and always right men
sick of sick men sick of sickness
Protestant- and Catholic-ness
sick of every lying bromide
Happy Birthday Merry Yuletide
freedom truth and brotherhood
Reader's Digest motherhood
pledge allegiance to the flag
"under God"—now what's the gag?

Sick of vicious ostentation
sick of humor's constipation
sick of sickness human sickness
human greed and human thickness.

Get my Brother off my back
White Red Yellow Brown and Black.
Perish Abel perish quick—
One of us is awful sick.

III

4:6-7

Why are you angry, why are you downcast?
If you do well, will you not be accepted?

If I do well? What do you mean by well?
I am the very symbol of respect.
You know me, J.B. Cain, the president
of Acme Company; presiding deacon
of my church. They say I *am* the church,
that no one moves a chair or spends a dime
belonging to the church without my knowledge
and my consent.

　　　　　　Or let me introduce
myself, Professor Cain. What can I say
but what is said: noted authority;
writer of books and brilliant articles;
dynamic lecturer, admired of students,
the envy of his colleagues. A modest man,
I live for learning and its meager fruits.
The adulation I but tolerate.
My one profession is the field of knowledge:
I spurn, for this career, all lesser goods.

If I do well? What do you mean by well?
I am a student here, one of the best.
Jonathan Cain the Third. I chose this school
(as did my father, Jonathan the Second
as did his father, Jonathan the First)

and was accepted here because I have
the proper gifts, the proper attributes.
Not only am I here, but I belong
(it is enough to say that I belong).
The contours of success are everywhere
apparent in my person and my station.
I am the son of parents who are right;
I am the product of the proper schools;
I am myself the rightest of the right.

If I do well? What do you mean by well?
Meet Luther Cain, the bright young minister.
Servant of God. I love thy kingdom, Lord,
the house of thy abode. I give myself
to thee and to thy church. And no mean gift
it is. I am an honor graduate
of Christian University where I
was student council president and triple
letter man. (They called me "Triple-threat"
not in the mundane football sense, but as
a triple threat in studies, sports, and love.)
I come to thee and to thy service, Lord,
equipped in mind and heart—and in physique.
Together we will lead thy people, Lord.

Why do you say to me, "If you do well"?
I am a doctor, lawyer, engineer.
I am a businessman, Rotarian.
I earn an honest wage, I pay my bills.
I give to feed the poor. I hate what must
be hated. I support the decent causes.
I am a Mason, thirty-third degree,
Knight of Columbus, Synagogue and Temple.
I am a Man, firstborn of Adam, son
of God, king of the universe. A Man!

If I do well—my God, what do you want?

IV

4:7   *If you do well, will you not be accepted?*

Acceptance is it now? You toss that out
as if it were a simple thing: do well
and be accepted. *Ganz einfach! Voila!*

It does not work that way. To be accepted
or not to be accepted is the question;
and if to be accepted, on what terms,
whose terms, by whom, with whom, and to what end?

I know you, Chief. I know your ancient problem.
The word about your nature gets around.
I know your universalistic leanings;
I know that you are gracious, merciful,
in anger slow, in steadfast love abounding.
This is, at least reputedly, the word.
This is your widely rumored reputation.
I hope you will not mind a mild rebuff:
deity should be made of sterner stuff.

You offer me acceptance, *on your terms*.
You will accept me—if I come with Abel.
And this is what you mean by doing well:
hold my revolting brother by the hand.

Let me propose the terms. If you want me,
you cannot have my brother. Damn it, God,
you know how rudely Abel comes between
the two of us. He fouls our sweet communion
where two is company and three's a crowd.
It is for you, for us, I cut him off!
Besides, my way is difficult enough,
my passage rough enough, my risky crossing
fraught enough with hazards of my own.

The choice to be or not to be accepted
is mine to make, and I have made the choice.
Acceptance on your terms is unacceptable:
As far as I'm concerned, Abel is dead.

V

4:8 *Let us go out into the field.* Come, Abel,
how shall I kill you? Let me count the ways,
since violence is versatile and knows
not only savage acts of massacre
by human malice or indifference,
but subtler forms as well, aesthetic forms
which spare the sight and smell of death and yet
remove the victim. Homicide can be,
on any scale, grotesque or beautiful.
Human community can be destroyed
in crude brutality or, if one will,
if one but exercise intelligence,
in fashion cold and clean and rational.

4:8 *So Cain rose up against his brother Abel
and killed him.* Yahweh said to killer Cain,
Where is your brother Abel? Where is Abel!
I do not know. Am I my brother's keeper?

VI

4:10
(RSV) *"What have you done? The voice of Abel's blood
is crying to me from the ground.* The voice
of Abel's blood, a thousand thousand voices
crying to me from the bloody ground!

29

"O Cain, my son, my son, who took the life
of Abel, son of mine. The voice of Abel,
the voice of Abel's blood, is crying to me
from the bloody ground, the blood-soaked ground.
O Absalom, my son, my son, who took
the life of Amnon, son of mine; the voice
of Amnon, Absalom, is crying to me
from the ground. O bleeding son of mine,
the son your brother (son of mine) despised;
my son rejected, smitten, and afflicted;
my son, my wounded son, my dying son,
subjected to the public ways of dying
and all the countless, private, hidden ways—
in battle, execution, inquisition;
in lethal oven or in lethal humor;
in lynching by the hand of brutal brother;
or brutal psychological exclusion;
and always wholesale murder by neglect.

"My son, my son! The voice of Abel's blood
is crying to me from the ground. O Christ,
O Jesus Christ, my son, my dying son!"

VII

4:11-12   *Now cursed from the ground are you . . . it shall*
          no longer yield its strength . . . a fugitive
          and wanderer upon the earth are you.

4:13   My punishment is more than I can bear.
       You curse me from the ground, the earth, the land;
       the lovely land, the land of habitation;
       the land of tent and temple, house and home;
       the land of sound and singing; land of meeting;

the land of school and market; land of loving;
the land of birth and death and living passion;
the land of seeing, speaking, hearing, touching.

You curse me from the ground, and earth becomes
a curse and all its fullness—father earth;
productive mother earth; familial earth;
sister of faith and hope; consoling brother
of anguish; patient aunt, indulgent, loving;
the uncle, bluff and crude and roughly hearty;
the frail grandparent, shrunken and unknowing,
but holding on to life and holding on;
the winsome cousin, gaily violating
the old taboos, and scorning inhibitions;
and tender lover, spouse, the close companion.

VIII

You curse me from the ground—you curse my life!
The lovely land becomes the loveless land;
relationships which ought to give support
are sour, insubstantial, charged with doubt;
the earth, the bloody earth, is unresponsive;
and I—I am a bitter fugitive,
a restless wanderer upon the earth,
cut off from Abel *and from you!*

From you,
you stubborn God! I can't lay hold of you!
From your face I am hidden. Where are you?

Take back your bloody earth, your alien earth,
your loveless, lonely, godforsaken land.
This life, this bleak reality, is more
than anyone can bear. So come sweet death!

IX

4:15   Then Yahweh put a mark on Cain, a mark
        on everyone, lest we forget that we
        are not our own but God's, made in God's image.
        So fugitives we are, God's fugitives;
        and wanderers we are, God's wanderers;
        until the day we learn to live as keepers,
        when restlessness will be resolved in rest,
        and lovelessness in love, and all estrangement
        will be at last redeemed in death.

X

                        Whose death?

        Whose son?

                        Whose brother?

                                        Come sweet death!

CHAPTER THREE

The Flood

Genesis 6–9

6:5-7 Yahweh saw that the wickedness of humankind was great in the earth, and that every inclination of the thoughts of their hearts was only evil continually. And Yahweh was sorry [for having] made humankind on the earth, and [was profoundly] grieved. . . . So Yahweh said, "I will blot out from the earth [all that] I have created—people together with animals and creeping things and birds of the air, for I am sorry that I have made them."

6:8-9 But Noah found favor in [Yahweh's eyes]. . . . Noah was a righteous man, blameless in his generation; Noah walked with God.

6:13—7:4 And God said to Noah, . . . "Make yourself an ark. . . . I will send rain on the earth for forty days and forty nights; and every living thing that I have made I will blot out from the face of the ground."

7:12, 21 The rain fell on the earth forty days and forty nights. . . . And all flesh died. . . .

8:13 [When] the waters were dried up from the earth. . . .

8:20-22 Noah built an altar to Yahweh. . . . And when Yahweh smelled the pleasing odor, Yahweh said, . . .
"As long as the earth endures,
    seedtime and harvest, cold and heat,
summer and winter, day and night,
    shall not cease."

9:20-21   Noah . . . was the first to plant a vineyard. He
drank some of the wine and became drunk, and he
lay uncovered in his tent. . . .

I

Genesis 6:5   And Yahweh saw the depth of human evil
upon the earth, that all the images
of mind and heart were constantly perverted.

6:6   And Yahweh looked in anguish at creation,
the creatures God had set alive and loved,
the splendid earth, the now-corrupted earth,
perverse, pernicious earth Yahweh had made;
and Yahweh was distressed and desolate.

Jeremiah
8:18-20
(RSV)   "My grief is beyond all healing, [and] my heart
is sick within me. [Hear] the cry [that rises
throughout]
the length and breadth of [this creation]:
"The harvest is past, the summer is ended,
and [still] we are not saved!" This wretched
sickness,
this deep affliction, waits in vain for healing.
Hear now the crying, sense the brutal hatreds,
assay the stench, the rotting human stench,
and estimate the epidemic anguish.

Jeremiah
8:21ff.   "For all the wounds of earth, my heart is
wounded."
I mourn. Dismay has taken hold on me.
Is there no balm in Gilead? Or Rome?
No healing in Geneva? Is there then

no therapy in Paris or Beijing;
in Washington or London or Berlin?
Is there no antidote in Bogotá,
Johannesburg, Calcutta or in Seoul,
Jerusalem or Baghdad or Beirut,
in Moscow or Manila or Madrid;
Belfast, Hong Kong, Tokyo, El Salvador?
Is there no balm in Gilead? Where, now,
physicians to attend this giant patient,
this earth, this sick creation, moribund,
but charging like the stricken, bleeding bull
to violent death? Is there no balm, no wisdom
compounded with compassion, and no love
sufficient for this mortal, earthly illness?"

II

Job 1:6f.

"I hear the Adversary coming now.
A busy and ambitious Son of God,
the quintessential gross male chauvinist."

"Ah, there you are, Eternal Majesty!
Dear Lord, kind Lord, and gracious Lord, I pray,
grant me a word with you, just for today."

"Whence have you come?" (as if I do not know).

"From going to and fro upon the earth,
from walking up and down the whole creation—
and may it please the King and Lord of all."

"What do you think?" (as if I do not know,
you thorny, suave, frustrated deity;
now here it comes, the charge that everything
awry in human history results,
of course, from my naive mismanagement).

35

"It is, O Lord, with infinite compassion
(in keeping with Our nature) that I roam
this sad creation. May I speak, O Lord,
in perfect candor (as befits Our station)?
Your great mistake in this abortive act,
this (be it said) exquisite formulation,
this enterprise so wondrously conceived
and executed (yes, indeed!): Your error
(and I speak with justified annoyance,
albeit with respect) is one of judgment.

"Earth is a mess (to call a spade a spade),
a godforsaken, catastrophic mess.
Precisely so, a godforsaken mess,
forsaken by the very God who made it.
Now hold our fire, let me finish—Sir.
I know, all of us know, about your Word,
your efficacious Word, the Word with power;
your Word in history, interpreting
(and possibly affecting or effecting)
particular events. All of us know.

"Your repertoire, of course, is out of balance;
you favor Palestinian events
and specialize in wonders wrought on water.
Look at your classic acts—the bringing up
of sickly little Israel from Egypt;
the founding of Davidic monarchy;
the bitter act of cataclysmic judgment
against your chosen people, contradicting
your own avowed intent; the re-creation
of Judah, a pale and sterile image
of what had been before. And then at last
(you have macabre tastes) your masterpiece,
the pièce de résistance, the mighty act
par excellence—a bloody crucifixion."

III

"A godforsaken, catastrophic mess!
Oh, you were there all right, it isn't that.

"All of us know (this is too obvious)
your tendency to hover, shall we say,
to brood upon earth's insolent estrangement.
But witness how you 'reign' in history.
It is, of course, your show; you give it meaning;
the whole vast operation feeds itself
upon your life and love, and is sustained
entirely by your will. Well, are you King
or slave? Assert yourself—or let it go!

"Your bourgeois notions of democracy
have now become the laughingstock of heaven.
You want to be *elected* God, you want
to reign by universal acclamation.
You entertain the ancient, feudal dream
of loving subjects in a loving kingdom
presided over by a loving ruler.

"They even talk about you in the heavenly host,
good-naturedly, of course, among themselves.
Some now refer to earth as Yahweh's folly.
I hear a few of them developing
the theme of Yahweh's yo-yo: 'You remember
the yo-yo Yahweh dotes upon . . . the job
complete with continents and mighty seas . . .
with tides and private, yellow satellite . . .
and creatures on its surface, little folk
who strut about, and play at being God. . . .
That yo-yo is defiant, mutinous,
and spinning on its own—or that is what
the crazy little creatures think and want . . .
and what does Yahweh do but brood and sulk,
and sit there grim and wounded, grieved and weeping.'

"Well, by the holy Word of God, how patient
are you supposed to be, how long in anguish?
You ape too much the weaker human virtues—
forgiveness, patience, love, and sweet compassion.
All these are female virtues, female fodder
in church and in the League of Women Voters.
Come, be a Man, for God's sake, be a Man.
Assume command! And act! Destroy the earth!"

IV

"Or, if to act in full annihilation
offends your godly love of rebel earth,
we'll simply for the moment dream a dream,
project a dream of total inundation
by which you start the earth again.

Genesis 6:8-9   "There's Noah.
Always there is the good and blameless Noah,
the gentle Noah, upright, righteous Noah
(whose name is also Job or Albert Schweitzer;
Mother or Saint Teresa, or Bonhoeffer;
or Daniel, Unamuno, short St. John;
or any of the thousands of the 'good').

"There's Noah over there, the peerless Noah,
the clean and honest Noah—noble Noah.
Wipe out the rest. Spare Noah, nifty Noah.
        Let God make another start,
        drawing from the pure in heart.
        God, become a remnant-maker:
        save the giver, drown the taker,
        drown the hater, spare the good,
        thus producing brotherhood.
        Suffering Lord and gentle Schemer,
        here's the dream—you be the Dreamer."

V

"A dream of yours, of course, is more than dream.
It always *is*, and in its dreadful *isness*
it teeters on the brink of history
or hangs, suspended by the merest thread,
above existence, threatening to fall
from dream to Word, from myth to dire fulfillment.
In *any* time of dreaming of this dream,
the dream *could* turn to stark reality.

"This dream of flood, by rain or radiation,
ozone depletion, garbage and pollution,
this dream of yours of lethal inundation—
this is a proper dream, *a proper act*
appropriate to the Maker and Sustainer
of life and earth and elemental nature,
as well as to secessionist creation.

"You and your silly notions of election!
The votes are being counted and the fact is
you haven't got a prayer. You're way behind
the leaders—Pentagons, Transnationals,
Trilateral Commissions, the elite
of humankind who *really* rule the earth.
You're even running second to some *Things:*
to Ships and Shoes and Sealing Wax and Cabbages;
to Institutions—Church and Bank and Bed.

"Now be a Man; for God's sake, be a Man.
Become a manly God and cut the thread.
Let fall the dream and bring for once and all
your anguish and *creation* to an end.

"And now, forgive me, Lord, if I have spoken
a word amiss. I speak, you know, in love."

VI

"Well, thank you, gentle Adversary. There,
the wind subsides, the mighty blow is gone
and I am God again—not 'man' nor male.

6:7   *I will blot out all of humanity*
       from off the earth . . . for I regret creation.

Did I dream this; and shall I dream it now?
Is there then nothing for it but to drown it,
to snuff it out, extinguish it, erase it—
this heedless, insubordinate creation,
this sick, estranged, rebellious, bleeding earth;
this life, this love, this long intoxication,
this cherished, fabulous, unique existence?

        "Shall I now begin to shout,
        Blow that stinking candle out!
        Drifting, derelict domain—
        bury it in lethal rain!

7:4   "Forty days and forty nights
        bury depths and bury heights,
        inundate the whole creation,
        every country every nation.
        Blot out everything with breath—
        perish life . . . and come sweet death.

"Wipe out the rest! Spare Noah, nifty Noah!"

VII

"And so, the dream, and I Yahweh, the dreamer.
Of course I ought to know (of course I know):

40

a self-perpetuating righteousness
exists in no one, let alone the race,
The dream goes wrong. What comes of all this rain,
this baptism, this death and resurrection?
What comes of this remarkable prescription
'Let God effect from righteousness (named Noah)
a new beginning: spark the ancient ruins
with nobleness and truth!' What comes of this?

9:20-25   "The gentle Noah soon is alcoholic,
and nakedness again becomes a problem.
8:21   The pleasing odor of the purged creation
begins again to reek of new pollution;
and we, the purged and Purger, folk and God,
are once again estranged. A sordid ending.
A somber, sorry, sordid new beginning.

VIII

"So let the dream of flood remain a dream.
I grieve in truth; but to assert control
I cannot go beyond my Word—the soft,
persistent Word, the Word that I have spoken
from time to time to some who know I speak
and some who do not know, but hear and speak
the Word again, unlabeled; paint the Word
or dance the Word or act the Word unmarked
and unidentified, but still the Word;
the Word made flesh, the Word by incarnation,
the Word that always *is*, however much
they try to say 'it was' or 'it shall be'!
Beyond the Word I cannot, will not, go."

IX

8:22   "While there is earth, while earth remains, these things
shall be: seedtime and harvest, cold and heat,
summer and winter, day and night—these things
shall be.

                    "And people, too—to feed the earth
and harvest it; to know and sense and savor,
to glory in and vehemently protest
the range and variation of the earth;
to make of it an idol or a demon;
to worship it or curse it; feel at one
with it, at home in it; or halting, stumbling
across its eyeless, unresponsive face
remain, as long as life remains, an alien
upon the earth, withdrawn, embittered, lonely.
As long as earth remains, these things shall be."

X

"But *I* shall be, my *Word* shall be, forever.
And what no lethal rain can bring about,
no righteousness effect, my Word shall do—
the Word that always is, the Word made flesh,
the Word of God Incarnate. . . . Come sweet death!"

CHAPTER FOUR

The Tower

Genesis 11

1-2 Now the whole earth had one language and the same words. And as [people] migrated from the east, they came upon a plain in the land of Shinar and settled there.

3 And they said to one another, "Come, let us make bricks, and burn them thoroughly." And they had brick for stone, and bitumen for mortar.

4 Then they said, "Come, let us build ourselves a city, and a tower with its top in the heavens, and let us make a name for ourselves; otherwise we shall be scattered abroad upon the face of the whole earth."

5-6 Yahweh came down to see the city and the tower, which mortals had built. And Yahweh said, "Look, they are one people, and they have all one language; and this is only the beginning of what they will do; nothing that they propose to do will now be impossible for them.

7 Come, let us go down, and confuse their language there, so that they will not understand one another's speech."

8-9 So Yahweh scattered them abroad from there over the face of all the earth, and they left off building the city. Therefore it was called Babel, because there Yahweh confused the language of all the earth; . . . and scattered them abroad over the face of all the earth.

I

At this time all the earth was of one speech
and common words. A treeless Eden.
A simple, single speech.
Contrast the present
babel.

II

They found a fertile valley in Shinar
and settled there. Shinar, is it?
or Shaker Heights or Shechem;
Sheboygan, Shanghai
Shiloh.

They talked among themselves of making brick.
"Come, burn the brick—it will endure—
and build the stalwart city
for us, ourselves.
For us.

"And let us make a tower for ourselves,
its head above all heights. And we
will scale the dizzying heights
ourselves, for us.
For us.

"We have at hand the stuff to join the brick.
So build it brick by burning brick,
a brick upon a brick.
The ruddy brick.
The Brick . . .

"All glory be to thee, O ruddy Brick,
almighty Brick that we have made,
O burned and burnished Brick,
our refuge and
our strength.

"This Brick, this mighty fortress, is our God,
a bulwark never, never failing;
our shelter from the flood
of mortal ills
prevailing.

"Ah blessed Brick that builds the steadfast city.
Ah wondrous tower, head in heaven.
On these we proudly stamp
our name—Produced
by Us.

"Security, the power to resist
dispersion—by Us: the means
of order and control
of destiny.
Amen."

III

Produced by Us—the rape of scores of cities
across the face of human history.
The ghastly inquisitions—Built by Us.
The ghettos, Jesus Christ, the bloody ghettos
Produced by Us; the rotten, stinking ghettos
in classic form a "Christian" institution
ordained, perpetuated, in the name
of Christ—O fraudulent appropriation!
The *barrios*, *favelas*, slums—all strewn

in hideous variety of form
across the loveless texture of the earth.

It is an ugly wonder that this One,
created in the image of Creator,
to be Oneself creator, turns One's hand
with vast creative passion, tirelessly,
to works of death. An ugly wonder, this.
The function of Creator is inverted:
no longer is it order out of chaos,
and light called forth from darkness, life from death;
but chaos out of order, dark from light,
and death from life. An ugly, morbid wonder.
One hears the timeless cry, demonic shout,
from breathing, feeling, living god-like beings,
from throats alive and lusty—"Long live Death!"

> A city and a tower and a name
> produced by Us, destroyed by Us,
> in ceaseless, senseless cycle.
> This pride of Ours
> is death.

IV

> Yahweh came down, who never sleeps or slumbers.
> God walks the Garden; loves the Brothers;
> acts, in Flood, in judgment;
> and knows the Tower
> is death.

> Yahweh came down. God comes. The life of God—
> participating, anguished life—
> impinges on existence
> (invoked or not)
> in love.

All silently and uninvoked God comes
to view the vast, pretentious city
and monumental tower
to human pride,
to pride!

God hears one calling to another, saying,
Luke 2:10-11 "Be not afraid; we have good news of joy,
great joy, to all of us. For unto us
is born this day a city and a tower.
Isaiah 9:6 The government shall be within the city
and We will make ourselves a name for Us—
Wonderful Counselor, Almighty God
and Everlasting Father, Prince of Peace!

Luke 2:12 "And this shall be a sign for us—the Tower,
the monumental Tower touching heaven."

Luke 2:13-14 And suddenly there is the multitude
of earthly hosts all praising Us and saying,
"Now glory be to You above the highest,
and in the city peace forevermore."

V

Genesis 2:7 "But it is I who breathe into your nostrils
the breath of life. Your breath is mine to give
or take away. I teach you how to walk,
not once upon a distant time, but now.
The step you take today you take with me.
You live and move and have your very being
in me, in my existence, in my life.
I always am, I AM, however much
you try to say I was—or never was.

Isaiah 29:16   "You turn things upside down! Will you regard
the potter as the clay? And is it right
for something made to say against the Maker,
'You made me not,' or something formed to say
to One who is the Former and Sustainer
of everything, 'You have no understanding'?

"Now see the wretched sum of it, this madness,
this monstrous folly of appropriation,
this mortal seizure of immortal power.
Your city and your tower become your tomb
when in your prideful dreaming I am dreamed
out of existence; when you put your trust,
your ultimate security, in that
which you have fashioned with your hands
    and mind."

VI

"Your name is Adam, falling from the tree,
the tower of your pride and independence,
in sight of lusty Eve. The Tower builder.

"Or Cain, who from the height of Abel's murder
slips off into an anguished life of falling,
in conscious, deadly, swift descent to death
upon the lusting earth, the bloody earth,
from whence your Brother's blood forever calls.
The Tower builder, Cain.

            "Or noble Noah,
the righteous Noah: from the mighty heights
above the Flood, descending to the earth
and sinking in the mire, the lusting mire.
Noah, Tower builder.
"Tower, Tower!"

Isaiah
2:12-17

"I have a day against all that is proud;
against all that is lifted up and high;
against all lofty things in nature which
become objects of human praise and worship—
    cedars of Lebanon
    oaks of Bashan
    all the high mountains
    and all lofty hills.
I have a day against all human pride,
against the posturing symbols of that pride—
    against the high towers
    and fortified walls
    against all the ships
    and magnificent craft!
And human haughtiness will be subdued
and human pride brought low. And I alone
will be exalted in that awful day."

VII

Exodus 3:14

Yahweh
"I AM" came down.
God comes. The life of God,
participating, anguished life,
impinges absolutely on our life.

The day
the awful day
is every day because
we cannot live by Things alone
but by the Word of judgment and redemption.

"Come then
let us go down
confusing there their speech
so that they cannot understand
the language of the city and the Tower."

VIII

So you can take it, God, and keep it, God,
this thwarted life, this frustrated existence.
A something quite describable is missing:
we do not really speak to one another;
we do not really see and read each other.
A something sweet and soft and warm, responding
in words, in speech, in plain communication
is missing, wanting, absent—or illusive:
always, O God, so damnably illusive—
a something that is something like a Word . . .

This punishment is more than we can bear.
You render one an alien from the other.
North has no Word for South, nor South for North.
Intelligible speech begins—and then
abruptly ends in empty, tortured words.
We talk across the wide proliferation
of human boundaries, uneasy borders,
from home and church to school and neighborhood.
We bellow in our rage, "Why is it, then,
so goddam hard to talk, to speak a word?"
We shout our syllables frenetically
as if a violent delivery
were substitute for simple understanding.
In all of this bewilderment of words
you make us fugitives and wanderers
among ourselves and even in ourselves.

This punishment is more than we can bear.

IX

Hosea 11:9   "I bear it too, I who am God, not 'man,'
the Holy One among you, in your midst.
I hear the cry from out the length and breadth

of this creation, sensing brutal hatreds
unmediated by communication.
I measure the immeasurable anguish
of Wordless words in endless mutual flow,
a frantic, empty, incoherent traffic.
But I am God, not 'man,' the Holy One
among you, in your midst. I will not come,
I will not visit you, in simple wrath.
In judgment there will always be redemption.

"I have a day against the high and lofty,
a day of execution, on a cross;
an awful day—a height against all heights:
a single, lonely, sickening, dizzying height
to which a Man has climbed, the Son of Man.
This too, like any height, betokens pride,
but not of earth: this is the pride of God.
Here too the pride of height is death; but now
this pinnacle of pride becomes unique,
for in descent again to lusty earth,
to bleeding earth, life is restored again
to Man and 'man,' the earth is soothed and healed,
the mire itself redeemed and life renewed."

X

Come Lord
Babel is better.
The Word of God is heard
in shattered pride; and from your fullness
we will all receive . . . grace upon grace.

So come
O come sweet death
O come Incarnate Word
O come, O come Immanuel
and ransom captive, Wordless Israel.

CHAPTER FIVE

The Land

Genesis 12 and 15

12:1 Now Yahweh said to Abram, "Go from your country and your kindred and your father's house to the land that I will show you.

12:2-4 I will make of you a great nation, and I will bless you, and make your name great, so that you will be a blessing. I will bless those who bless you, and the one who curses you I will curse; and in you all the families of the earth shall be blessed." So Abram went, as Yahweh had told him. . . .

15:6 And he believed Yahweh, [who] reckoned it to him as righteousness.

I

Okay, Yahweh. Let's recapitulate.
Creation we can take, after a fashion—
the proposition that the cup of life,
Psalm not, incidentally, always overflowing,
23:5 is given to us by Another: You;
Yahweh; Creator; Ground of Being; God;
the Source, the unknown Source; the unknown Giver.
You thought that we would know you from the gift,
that we would see you in the cup?
My God, it's hard enough to see ourselves!

Our grasp of the cup is uneasy, unsteady:
the handle is awkward, the contents too heady.
We juggle the cup holding falcon and dove,
with a fist of oppression in white nylon glove.

II

OK, Yahweh. Let's recapitulate.
You gave the cup—not quite without a word,
but nothing more. An unobtrusive word,
a quiet word, sometimes a silent word.
And, we confess, we don't know how to drink.
We cannot take this stuff you give.

Jeremiah 8:22,
11
Psalm 19:3,
4

            Look back
across our years. There *is* no balm, no peace.
There is no common speech or language heard,
no voice, cohesive line, throughout the earth.
Our drunkenness unleashes flood upon
destructive flood on all of us. We drink
the cup and, stinko, make of all our sweet
and perilous encounters only Babel.

III

OK, Yahweh. Let's recapitulate.
In certain areas we've achieved finesse,
sophistication past imagination.
But God!—what most we need, we haven't got.
    We land people on the moon;
    our computers are a boon;
    (but we can't transform the ugly faces
    of our cities' vilest places).
    We've got ready to release

what it takes to make wars cease—
   What ain't we got?
   We ain't got peace.
We've got skill to sight the blind,
ways to heal the fractured mind
(while we covet neighbor's house
and we sleep with neighbor's spouse).
We've got God-in-heaven above
and the voice of turtledove—
   What ain't we got?
   We ain't got love.

IV

OK. So much for recapitulation.
So here we are, a new church generation,
new-minted in the new theology
(whatever that may be); fresh-coined, bold
in new experimental liturgy,
aware of all the brave new forms designed
to make the gospel come alive again.

(And parenthetically one wants to add:
whatever be the verdict of the doctors
on whether God is dead, or mutilated;
or maybe somehow sick—this allegation
of critical divine pathology—
whatever be the fact, while we inquired,
the Holy Spirit seemingly expired.)

Let us be truthful, God, since we affirm
no secrets hide from you; let us be frank.
We're scared. We're playing with a deck that's stacked.
The odds seem hopelessly against us now.
In faith we're called to take this whole sick world

as adversary, subject of our conquest.
And we go forth to battle, armed to teeth
with puny theological peashooters,
supported by a Word from you, itself
so unobtrusive as to warrant doubt.
We're scared. We're frightened at the *sound* of you!
We think the trumpet-voice, blasting our ears,
or silence, utter silence, would be better.

Isaiah "Whom shall I send, and who will go for us?"
6:8 The question rings about as strong and true
as gramophone recordings of Caruso;
and our response, "Well, here we are, send us,"
is equally distorted, unconvincing.
We hear ourselves, unreal and automated,
our voices thin, devoid of resonance,
and wonder at this strange exchange,
this dreamlike insubstantial confrontation
between the called and Caller, both of whom
seem frail at best. Or worse, we play a game,
we stage a farce of mutual deception.

V

Isaiah's temple vision better suits
an age of quieter piety than ours.
Our temples are too busy doing the work
of temples; much too noisy in the task
of making temple sounds. Our temples temple.
From morning until night, frenetically,
they go about the busy work of templing.
We haven't anything against Isaiah.
It's only that we've got a *thing* with temples.

And there's another reason why we can't
authentically appropriate the vision:
our minds are much too busy being minds,
and much too noisy making thinking sounds.
From morning until night, frenetically,
we celebrate the work of cerebration.
We do not want to listen and respond.
We want to take command. We want to work,
manipulate, and cerebrate the Word.
In any case, the *hearing* of the Word
comes hard for us. The time, at least, is wrong.
In any case, Isaiah's vision suits
some other epoch better than our own,
some other age, some other generation.

VI

OK, Yahweh. Consider Abraham,
that legendary ancestor whose life
is told in ancient Israel in terms
appropriate to what that chosen people
then deemed their chosenness to mean and be.
The story of old Abraham was shaped
by Israel's corporate sense of entity
imposed upon a single man. The call
of Abraham is more than personal.
In Israel's faith, this is the Call *in essence*.

Genesis 12ff.   The lie he told is everyone's deceit,
his greed, his lust, his self-concern are ours;
his crass unfaith, committed as it were
in the same breath with fervent affirmation,
is our unfaith; and his redemption, frail
and frangible, repeatedly in doubt,

assaulted vehemently by acts of pride,
is ours. The "partriarch" is everyone.

We're clear on this, Yahweh, and you must be.
I thought it well for you to know that we
all understand the nature of the text.

VII

Okay. This is the essence of the call.

Genesis 12:1   The *language* of the call? "Go from your country,
and from your kindred and your parents' house.
Go to the land that I will show you!"

              Great!
If we can read you straight and take the words
at superficial value—it's a breeze,
a cinch. No sweat. Who wants to live at home?
Who wants to live it all in Austinburg,
in Walton, Marion, or Cheverly?
Who wants to live and die in Lexington,
or Brooklyn, Pittsburgh, Closter, Menlo Park?
Who here aspires to go back home again?
Who wants to be a prophet without honor?

We are, Yahweh, the go-go generation,
and distant fields, in any case, are greener.

(But parenthetically you'll let me say:
if you expect to move us any distance,
you'll see that transportation is provided.
The move that Abram made to climes more sunny
was fine for Abraham: he married money.)

VIII

Okay, Yahweh? I know, it's not Okay.
It would be nice to take it so, so nice—
just break away and let you do the driving.
While we suspect the TV "church" of fraud,
they sometimes make it seem to us alluring;
and while we know it isn't all that simple,
sometimes the fundamentalists look good:
they have the straight, unvarnished Word of God.
The scheme is clear—no ambiguities.
Just leave, and God will take you to the land.
Accept the Lord and Savior, Jesus Christ
today, right now; and Peace, you're in the land.
Don't fornicate: you're in the land. Don't drink:
you're there. And read the Bible every day.
You'll have the overflowing cup of life,
the cup of grace, elixir, in the land.
And guard with care your own sweet soul's salvation—
you're in the land, the land is yours, the land
of milk and honey! Praise the Lord!

                    Oh yes.
Just one thing more. You'll want to *stay*, of course;
so keep it clean and personal. Don't foul
your antiseptic faith with politics
(unless, of course, it's widely to the right);
don't mess in messy social enterprises.
You know the Word of God—it's in the Book—
give Caesar what is Caesar's. *Give God God's!*
And so, be fruitful in the promised land,
the land the Lord thy God hath given thee.

God, what a land! A lousy, lying land;
a dirty, stinking, bleeding, schizoid land!
Lord Jesus Christ, that's where we *are*, that's where

we've *been*. That's where we *started*. That's the land
from which you call us out, the very land
of "country, kindred, land of father's house!"

IX

Okay, Yahweh. We know it will not wash.
Where is the land to which you want to lead us,

**Genesis
12:2-3**

endow us with a name, and make us great;
and bless the ones who bless us, curse our cursers;
and let *us* bless the families of the earth?
Where is this never-never land, Yahweh,
and where are you?—except in Jesus Christ.
We have to go and go and go and go,
perhaps not going anywhere, but going;
we have to go and go, and find the land,
and occupy the land—and *never* know,
and never *know* that we are in the land.

We lose the land, as ancient Israel learned,
when we possess the land, and claim the land,
and name the land, and call the land our own.

X

The land is come upon in doing the work,

John 1:1ff.

redemptive work, of him who is the Word,
the unobtrusive Word, the quiet Word,
sometimes, it seems, the silent, hidden Word.

The land belongs to Christ, whose name is ours;
whose greatness we appropriate in love;

who, only, has the power of curse and blessing,
but by whose grace it can be given us
to bless the families of the earth.

Come, Christ,
in us!
Come fresh again, sweet death, in us!
And in our dying from the ancient land,
bring us by our sweet death into the Land.

PART
TWO

*Time of
Burning*

The Burning in the Midst

Exodus 1–4

I

Exodus
1:1, 5-7

These . . . came to Egypt with Jacob, . . . seventy [persons].
Joseph was already in Egypt. Then Joseph died, and all
his brothers, and that whole generation. But the Israelites
were fruitful and prolific; they multiplied and grew
exceedingly strong, so that the land was filled with them.

So, many score and some-odd years ago
our founders brought forth on this continent
another national entity conceived,
so we have all been told, in liberty
and dedicated to the proposition,
so we have all been schooled, that one is one,
each one created equal to another,
and everyone—this always was implicit—

to live in freedoms to and freedoms from:
freedom to find and be and rule oneself;
freedom from any kind of tyranny
of mind or body, any subtle kind
of thought manipulation, any brand
of native North-American pharaohism.

Maybe it wasn't Egypt at the start—
so many score and some-odd years ago—
since Egypt is another name for bondage,
and we were free.

             Or that's our recollection.
But can we know a past, especially one
that's celebrated, ritualized, and made
a kind of cultic act, its distant smoke
inhaled, refined, through purifying filters?
It really wasn't Egypt then—at least
so speaks the ritual myth. The land was free.
But then our Joseph died, our Washington,
our Jefferson, our own staunch patriarchs.
Descendants of our Israel were fruitful;
they multiplied and slowly filled the land.
And we were joined, as Israel was joined,
by some who came to Israel as slaves
and some who came in hope of promised lands.
The land was filled with us. The cities now
were overrun with us. America
the Beautiful becomes the land of Egypt.

  O beautiful for smoggy skies,
     For washing of the brain,
  For hillsides stripped of majesties,
     For strontium in rain.
  Imperial America,
     Thy power preys on thee,
  And damns the good of neighborhood
     From sea to oily sea.

So many score and some-odd years ago.
It really wasn't Egypt then—at least
so speaks the ritual myth; The land was free.
Look, for example, at the campus scene.
The country and the campus then were clean:
John Harvard first in sixteen thirty-six;
William and Mary, sixteen ninety-three;
Old Elihu supplying Yale a name
still years before the birth of Washington.
But then, however true the ritual myth,
however pure and free the origins,
establishments of higher learning, like
the sons of Jacob, grew exceeding strong,
were fruitful, multiplied—and filled the land.

II

Exodus 1:8   *Now there arose up a new king over Egypt, which knew*
(KJV)   *not Joseph.*

                    Egypt now is Egypt,
          since Egypt is the state of namelessness,
          of heedlessness, of human deprivation,
          of making us not simply less than God
          but less than humankind in psyche, mind.
          Joseph's descendants lose identity
          except as his descendants. Persons are
          depersonned, losing face by being faceless,
          reduced from "thou" to "it," from personhood
          to function, category, type, profession;
          from separate, total human entity
          to functionaries in the national temple.

          Even within the university
          the single person now was lost. Of course.

The student populations grew from tens
to hundreds, thousands, even tens of thousands.
William and Mary's campus progeny,
like Jacob's sons and daughters, are confined
to purposes defined by Pharaoh's will.

And so, the age-old question sounds again:
Is Pharaoh made for us or we for Pharaoh?
Who serves whose purposes? Who said, "sabbath
was made for us, not we for sabbath"? Or,
who said, how many times, to all the forms
of Pharaoh—corporate, institutional,
political—now let my people go?

III

Exodus 1:9ff.
(paraphrased)

*"Look," Pharaoh said to his people, "these people,
the children of Israel, have become so numerous
and strong that they are a threat to us. We must
be prudent. If war should break out, they might
add to the number of our enemies. They might
escape out of the country." Accordingly, the
Egyptians forced the Israelites into slavery, and
made their lives unbearable with hard labor, work
with clay and with brick, all kinds of work in the
fields.*

Stay
with clay.
Stick
to brick.
The system yields
to work in the established fields.
When the boys come out to play
keep your faith in yesterday.

Avoid the whip, eschew the lash,
and don't complain about the hash.
Those who do it Pharaoh's style
will be around for quite a while.

IV

Exodus 3:1ff. *Now Moses led his flock to Horeb, the mountain of God.*
(paraphrased) *And lo, a bush was burning yet it was not consumed.*
And Moses said, "I will turn aside and see this great
sight, why the bush is not burnt." And God called to
him from the midst of the bush, "Moses, Moses!" And
he said, "Here am I." Then God said, "Put off your
shoes from your feet, for the place on which you are
standing is holy ground."

So call us Moses. Here we are at Horeb.
The Holy Mountain is the Holy Church:
or is it Holy University;
or Holy Bank; or Holy Corporation?
Whatever be our private sanctuary,
the Egypt of the world is far-removed
from us. The oppressive ways of Pharaohism
need not disturb us here. Our various priests
in Academe, priests of the God of Learning;
or churchly priests, dispensing full support
for status quo which is our meat and drink;
or priests in Washington, apparently
with access to the oracle of God—
in any case, our priests are able to
defend us from all ills in this bleak world.
Who cares about the next?

And if we live
as good communicants—in Academe

in sober worship of the God who rules
the land of academic discipline,
where one drinks deep from wells of mathematics
and science, engineering, geophysics;
where one digests the proffered, packaged past
of all our long-accumulated treasures,
of all our stunning, sordid, devious ways;
if in the Church without examination
we take the easy faith; if in this land
we play the nation's power games with zest—
then great will be the ultimate rewards:
a safe profession, ever larger flocks
and herds, security and private order
amidst the wide world's insecurity,
oppression, poverty, injustice, death.

V

But what will we do with the bush, my friend,
   O what will we do with the bush?
What do we make of the fire that burns,
   but fails to consume what it burns?
What will we say to the voice that we hear
   from out of the heart of the fire?
What do we answer the Word that calls "Holy"
   the ground of the burning,
   the ground of our standing?
And what do we say to the call out of burning,
the call out of "Egypt" and Baghdad and Basra;
El Chorrillo (it happened that Panama Christmas);
Nicaragua; Granada; Allende in Chile;
the screams of Vietnam and the cries of Korea;
Guatemala's Arbenz; and now soon to be heard from,
Coca fields of Colombia and of Peru?
So what do we say to these calls from our burnings,

the call from our sisters, the weeping of brothers?
What will we do? That crazy bush is burning.
That Voice is calling, "This is Holy Ground!"
Your place and time are holy; set apart—
but not for refuge from the mortal storm.
If this is what you want, then close your ears,
and turn your back, and walk away.
Refuse to see the bush, deny the Voice,
and shut yourself away from human bondage.

The burning bush, the Voice, the Word, remain.
Look close to see what burns without consumption:
the bitterness of interhuman hate
is in the fire, unconsumed; cities
are burning; smugness and hypocrisy,
conformity and apathy still burn;
the noxious gas of all our national jargon
still feeds the fire;
                    and poverty;
                               and war.

And if we do not turn away, the Voice
and Word are clear out of the burning bush.
Our Horeb is accursed if it becomes
in any way at all a sanctuary,
an isolated academic tower,
or pious theological retreat
or fortress held to be impregnable;
if it is deemed to give us special tenure;
if Pharaoh's victims are ignored, if "Egypt"
is abandoned, . . . and the burning burns.

VI

The burning burns. It isn't Scotland burning.
It's not the city dump. The burning bush,

with inexhaustible supplies of fuel,
is humankind, incinerating flesh,
the corporate species, from the start till now
engaged in what would seem to be a sort
of diabolical self-immolation.
The powerful believe that they survive—
a rank deceit. Their own integrity,
their own humanity, are first to burn;
and what remains makes mockery of all—
a mean, distorted image of creation.

It is some kind of irreducible,
irrefutable gut theology
that puts God in the center of the burning:
"God called to Moses from inside the bush."
When will we learn that any Word of God
dissociated from the human scene
is fraudulent? The Word of God in prophet
is always in the midst of human burning;
the Word of God in Christ comes in the heat
of searing tears and burning blood and flesh
of incandescent *people*. Christ and prophet,
Word and Voice, the old and new I AM,
are truly heard from in the midst
of all our tortured human conflagrations.

VII

Exodus
3:10-11
(RSV)

*[God said to Moses,] "Come, I will send you to
Pharaoh that you may bring forth my people, the sons
of Israel, out of Egypt." But Moses said to God,
"Who am I that I should go . . . ?"*

Come off it, God! I'm not the one for this.
I like it cool. What kind of fireball God

are you? We've speculated all these years
about your nature; now I think you must
be made of pure, ineffable asbestos.
But what *you* have to bear in mind is that
your humble servant whom you take to be
a Moses-type, is really made of stuff
highly combustible. You'll let me say,
again, I like it cool.

        And furthermore,
I've got it made, since I can make the grade;
and since I have the very best credentials.
You want these days and years at my own Horeb
to point me back into the human fires
that burn around the nation and the world.
Go find someone with less at stake than I,
someone with less to lose. And will you move
your fireball presence somewhere else, or come
away from hiding in that burning bush?
The Lord be with you, Lord. I'm not the one!
I've got it made. I like to keep it cool.
I'll stay and gather rosebuds while I may,
and cash them in to keep your world at bay.

VIII

You won't take "no"? You say, "I will be there
with you." Ah, there's the rub!

        Now listen, Friend,
I'll tell it like it is. A lot of us
have wished to see you dead, and some of us
have tried to bury you by declaration.
It isn't for the petty stuff—I mean
the allegations of your looks, your place

in heaven, the strictly human attributes
by which you are effectively diminished.
I'm trying to say, I do not really think
we wish you dead because the talk of you,
the human talk of God, so often comes
from pious folk who twist you into forms
of their own prejudice and piety.

Your most intelligent, discerning foes,
your strongest opposition, really come
not now from those who deem your presence here
to be irrelevant, though this they claim.
It is your very relevance, the weight
of your direct impingement on our burning;
it is the overwhelming cost to us
of your excruciatingly direct,
your absolutely relevant, demands.

We do not fault *you* for the fusillade
of petty bullets fired from some quarters
of Christendom, the impotent barrage
of popcorn shot from moralistic guns.
It's simply that we cannot tolerate
the very *name* of you, because your name
is justice, love, compassion—qualities
we cannot bring to bear upon our times
without surrendering the cherished ways
that make *us* little gods upon the earth.

I like it here. Don't plague me with the plagues
of time and history. I like it here.
I like the perquisites, fringe benefits,
of my own special privilege. I can
avoid the burning bush.

And you.

And neighbor.

IX

In Exodus 4—the closing scene of his call—Moses,
still resisting, asks in effect to be further persuaded.
So Yahweh asks Moses, "What is that in your hand?" "A
staff," Moses says. "Throw it on the ground," Yahweh
commands; so Moses throws his staff on the ground and
it turns into a serpent.

But when, at the command of the Word, he catches it,
it becomes a staff again. He is told to put his hand
under his clothes against his chest. When he draws it
out it is covered with leprosy. At the command of the
Word, he repeats the gesture and his hand is restored.
Finally, water which he takes from the river turns to
blood when he pours it out on the ground. The saga
does not tell us so, but the parallel inference is
clear: at the command of the Word, spilled blood can
be turned back to fresh water, death can be turned
back again to life.

The Word speaks now to Moses and to us:

Look at the "miracles" of humankind,
the fabulous magicians. See them take
the structures of support, and by their magic
turn them into instruments of death.
Their brilliant, twisted alchemy makes sickness
where there was health, disease where human wholeness.
And wonder of all miserable wonders,
these wonder-working folk possess the power
to take life-giving water, flowing, fresh,
and pour it on the ground in blood and death.

We can revise their magic, you and I.
We can effect the countermiracle.
The venomous, unleashed, can be contained

in structures that support all human life.
The programmed, calculated brokenness
of life can be restored, our health revived.
And we can turn the tide of death to life.

X

**Exodus 4:10-12
(NJB)**

*Moses said to Yahweh, "Please, my Lord, I have
never been eloquent, even since you have spoken to
your servant, for I am slow and hesitant of speech."
"Who gave a person a mouth?" Yahweh said to him.
"Who makes a person dumb or deaf, gives sight or
makes blind? Is it not I, Yahweh? Now go, I shall
help you speak and instruct you what to say."*

CHAPTER TWO

The Burning in the Temple

Introduction to Isaiah 6

The call of Isaiah took place more than twenty-seven centuries ago. That prophet had an exceptionally long life and ministry, extending over the reigns of at least four kings of his country, Judah. Isaiah was an urbanite, living in what was for him and his people *the* city, Jerusalem. His language, his politics, and even his theology are impressively shaped by his urban existence.

And he is a man highly placed in Jerusalem, either by virtue of professional status or possibly by royal birth or by both. King Ahaz listens to him, if he does not heed him; and King Hezekiah, by any standard one of Judah's most distinguished kings, not only listens and heeds, but is strongly dependent on Isaiah.

I suppose we would have to say that none of the great Old Testament prophets is typical. Each is so powerfully unique. But no prophet represents classical prophetism more forcefully, more comprehensively, more eloquently, than Isaiah. He is, in the best sense of the word, the most sophisticated of the prophets. But it is finally his own honest, unneurotic, thoroughly realistic appraisal of himself and his own generation together with his historical and immediate knowledge of the

Word of God in time, Holiness, the Holy One in our midst, that create the essence of Isaiah's distinction.

Verses from Isaiah 6:1-12 (NJB)

In the year of King Uzziah's death I saw the Lord seated on a high and lofty throne; his train filled the sanctuary. Above him stood seraphs, each one with six wings: two to cover its face, two to cover its feet and two for flying; and they were shouting these words to each other:

> Holy, holy, holy is Yahweh Sabaoth
> His glory fills the whole earth.

The door-posts [some translations read "foundations"] shook at the sound of their shouting, and the Temple was full of smoke. Then I said:

> "Woe is me! I am lost,
> for I am a man of unclean lips
> and I live among a people of unclean lips,
> and my eyes have seen the King, Yahweh Sabaoth."

Then one of the seraphs flew to me, holding in its hand a live coal which it had taken from the altar with a pair of tongs. With this it touched my mouth and said:

> "Look, this has touched your lips,
> your guilt has been removed
> and your sin forgiven."

(And this is all we know or hear of seraphs. They appear nowhere else in Hebrew Scripture. The Hebrew root has to do with "burning.")

I then heard the voice of the Lord saying:

"Whom shall I send? Who will go for us?"

And I said, "Here am I, send me." He said:

> "Go, and say to this people,
> 'Listen and listen, but never understand!
> Look and look, but never perceive!'
> Make this people's heart coarse,
> make their ears dull, shut their eyes tight,
> or they will use their eyes to see,
> use their ears to hear,
> use their heart to understand,
> and change their ways and be healed."

(It is clear that Isaiah is looking back on the experience of his Call from a point much later in his ministry when it seems to him that his own prophetic career has only served to make his people more obdurate.)

I then said, "Until when, Lord?" He replied, "Until towns are in ruins and deserted, houses untenanted and a great desolation reigns in the land."

It is Isaiah who speaks first; then the Reverend Doctor Winner; and finally, briefly, Davie Napier.

It is Isaiah speaking now. Not in the year that King Uzziah of Judah died—about 740 B.C. Not more than twenty-seven hundred years ago. But now.

I

> It is the year that King Uzziah died.
> That's any year—for kings and queens are dying;
> since any child of earth is child of God,

born to be free, born to enhance the earth.
My God, we go on killing them like flies;
potential queens and kings, the kids that perish,
puking away their short-lived animation;
starved or exposed; or caught by rampant wars
imposed by those who would be emperors,
restraining multitudes from exercising
their given rights to live as folk of God.

These are the years when unsung queens and kings
are dying, sacrificed to feed the arrogance
of emperors concerned (they say) to save
(they say) the world (they say) from "terrorists"
(they say). And they, these mighty emperors,
will save the world, by God, if saving means
destruction.

See these years of dying kings,
of short-lived little queens—the third-world poor
deprived of crown of God and dispossessed
of status.

II

See the year of emperors
whose law and order function to preserve
the rights and perquisites—of emperors.

The emperors, in flesh of every shade,
appear in many lands and capitals,
hold office in establishments of law
and labor, government and education—
the emperors deprive God's queens and kings,
God's royalty, created in God's image,
of life, or human status, dignity—
and make each year a year of royal death.

III

It is the year that King Uzziah died.
I see the Lord. Well now, that's stretching things.
No one sees God, for heaven's sake. If God
is God she's not accessible to view
by any kind of pious peeping Tom—
be that one prophet, priest, or even saint.

If now we talk of sensing Holiness;
if we suspect an unexpected Presence;
if from the lips of seraphs never seen
before or since or, in the normal way
of apprehending, even now, we think
we hear a Word of Glory in the earth;
if we are sensitive to mystery;
if in the private place of our own being
we freshly sense the possibilities
of life, of new creation, restoration—
we know it has to do with death and burning,
and with our apprehension of the loss
of royalty.

          It is against the fact
of death, the scene of human unfulfillment;
it is against the knowledge of our woe,
the recognition of the sucking vacuum
of all our inhumanity that we,
among the world's sophisticated folk,
have intimations that our world of death,
our place of bleak unholiness, can be
invaded by the glory of the Holy.

These are the years of King Uzziah's death,
the time when royalty of God is crushed,
when folk conceived to be a little less
than God, are less than folk. This is a time
of shaking of foundations—and a time
of burning.

IV

When the realm of humankind
is not a realm but rather more a prison,
a form of tight, inhibiting restraint
of realization of humanity;
when our existence, when the very temple
that is our total corporate habitation
is shaken to its deepest substructure,
its long-submerged supports, its cornerstones;
and when our house, this earthly tabernacle,
is filled with smoke of our incineration—
our burning anger, bitterness, frustration,
our burning hate, humiliation, hunger,
our burning pride, consuming self-concern,
our burning psyche and our burning flesh—
When all of this occurs, and it is now,
it is a time of Calling . . . and a time
of certainty that Holiness is here.

V

Of course, you may deny all this, insist
you do not read this season of our life
this way. You may be one who listens, hears,
but never understands, who looks and sees,
refusing to perceive. You may deny
the shaking of the world's foundations, smoke
from human conflagrations. You may be
an emperor, contemptuous of queens and kings
who would be folk of God. If so
your temple is a miniature illusion,
your sanctuary is a private place
complete with garden for a ghostly walk,
an unreal, insubstantial tête-à-tête
among the dew-kissed roses. You will let me
wish you and your non-Jesus Jesus well.

The time of burning is the time of calling.
The knowledge, the acknowledgment, that we
are reeling in a deeply shaken world
opens the eye and ear to Holiness,
to Glory in the earth. The awful sense
that we are all unclean, immersed in death,
makes possible the vision of *the* King.

VI

Some see the vision in another way,
Some read this matter very differently.
I yield the floor to Reverend Doctor Winner,
no doubt of Norman stock, invincible
(and largely unconcerned with sexist speech).

"What is this talk of death? Isaiah lies.
To be a king, a living king, one has
but to confront oneself with fortitude.
One must resolve to think in positive,
affirmative, American, red-white-and-blue,
conformist, nonradical, (nonbiblical?),
autohypnotic terms.

"Isaiah's call should read: It was the year
that King Uzziah died. Poor man, he failed
to use the formula sufficiently.
He failed to tell himself repeatedly,
feet squarely planted, shoulders back, facing
his mirror with a smile, 'Kings never die!'
How should Isaiah's calling read? The year
of fire and death; the shaking of the Temple
of human habitation; burning time
in human history—maybe. But this
is not for me. It is for lesser men.

For I am in Jerusalem a man
of privilege, admired, accepted, loved;
a man of parts, acquainted with the ways
of royalty. As one to whom men turn
in hope, I am upheld in high esteem.

"Why should I bear the griefs and carry sorrows
of other men? Why let myself be hurt?
Why carry wounds of other men's transgressions;
and why be bruised for their iniquities?

"Or why, indeed, be called? I'll be the Caller!
Let other men protest of unclean lips
and take for cure the purifying fire.
I'm not about to be an errand boy
of Holiness!

       "It is the year of death
and I resolve that with the help of me,
myself, and my resources, I will live.
I will believe in me, myself, and so
should you. Now, suddenly, I see myself
upon a lofty throne. I know my strength,
I stamp upon my mind indelibly
the vivid image of my own success.
And it is I who say, 'Who now will go
for us?' and God responds, 'I'm here. Use me.'"

VII

So runs the version of the call revised
by Doctor Winner, and affirmed, endorsed
by clean, white, Anglo-Saxon Protestants
as well as all the confident Twice-Born
who think they have it made, or want to think

they have it made, by virtue of their own,
their very private merit; who believe
that God who knows a good thing when she sees it
is standing by them ready to respond,
and make of any untoward situation
an instant Camelot—for them, of course,
and other proper members of the faith.

VIII

These are the days of dying queens and kings,
when folk, born to be folk, are less than folk.
The sacrificial altar fire is burning.
Foundations shake. And we are all unclean.
But if we listen with prophetic ears,
within the smoke-filled temple of our world
the seraphs still are calling, burning calls
to burning, strangely not of death but life,
not of despair, but hope, and not of shame
but glory. Burning cries of holiness,
invading all of our unholiness,
as Christ, the son of God, the son of man,
the king—unceasingly invading time,
incessantly enduring crucifixion—
proclaims the ultimate but, in a sense,
already present rule of peace and justice.

IX

If you are burned by burning, intimate
with altar fires; if your own lips are seared
with burning coals from sacrificial altars;

if crucifixion—once for all in Christ
or in the bloody stream of human history—
if crucifixion of the son of "man"
fully impinges on your consciousness,
then you will not be able to escape
the Calling of the Caller; you will know
that you are called, called irresistibly,
without a word of promise of success;
called out against insuperable odds
to go and speak and work and live, in faith
that judgment must be finally redemptive,
that fire ultimately purifies,
that burning is for cleansing and forgiveness,
that love and righteousness and holiness
in fact pervade this shattered habitation.

And you and I are called to live in love
and affirmation of a burning world,
in confidence that corporate guilt is purged,
our corporate want of cleanness is forgiven;
that even if the smoke is never cleared
a Holiness invades our wanton violence
and Glory fills the anguish of our times.

X

The year that King Uzziah died: a time
of burning, time of shaking, time of calling.
"Whom shall I send and who will go for us?"
And I say, trembling like a slender reed
before the hurricane, in hope alone
of love and affirmation, confidence—
I say, "I think I'm here. Send me."

CHAPTER THREE

The Burning in the Bones

Verses from Jeremiah 1, 20, and 8

1:1, 2 The words of Jeremiah, son of Hilkiah, of the priests who were in Anathoth in the land of Benjamin, to whom the word of Yahweh came in the days of King Josiah son of Amon of Judah. . . .

1:5-8 "Before I formed you in the womb I knew you,
and before you were born I consecrated you;
I appointed you a prophet to the nations."
Then I said, "Ah, Yahweh God! Truly I do not know how to speak, for I am only a boy." But Yahweh said to me,
  "Do not say, 'I am only a boy';
  for you shall go to all to whom I send you,
  and you shall speak whatever I command you.
  Do not be afraid of them,
  for I am with you to deliver you,"
    says Yahweh.

1:9-10 Then Yahweh put out his hand and touched my mouth; and Yahweh said to me,
  "Now I have put my words in your mouth.
  See, today I appoint you over nations
    and over kingdoms,
  to pluck up and to pull down,
  to destroy and to overthrow,
  to build and to plant."

20:7-9 Yahweh, you have enticed me,
  and I was enticed;
you have overpowered me,
  and you have prevailed.
I have become a laughingstock
  all day long;
  everyone mocks me.
For whenever I speak, I must cry out,
  I must shout, "Violence and destruction!"
For the word of Yahweh has become for me
  a reproach and derision all day long.
If I say, "I will not mention him,
  or speak any more in his name,"
then within me there is something like a burning fire
  shut up in my bones;
I am weary with holding it in,
  and I cannot.

8:18-19*a* My joy is gone, grief is upon me,
  my heart is sick.
Hark, the cry of my poor people
  from far and wide in the land.

20-22 "The harvest is past, the summer is ended,
  and we are not saved."
For the hurt of my poor people I am hurt,
  I mourn, and dismay has taken hold of me.
Is there no balm in Gilead?
  Is there no physician there?
Why then has the health of my poor people
  not been restored?

I

Suppose we play the role of Jeremiah.
Suppose we take his part, assume his stance,
appropriate his point of view. Our world
becomes his world, our time and people his.

And we are Jeremiah, called by God
or Yahweh, called by Zeus or Allah, called
by unseen Spirit, Voice, or Word of One
who was and is and evermore shall be;
the Source and Sustenance of life and love;
Existence that is nonexistent—THOU
the Inescapable, in every "I"
and "you" and "she" and "he" and "we" and "they."

II

We're Jeremiah. More than most, we are
gregarious, and more than most we know
the longing to be heard, accepted, loved.
Intensely *people* people, we would like
to speak the smooth, the sparkling, pleasing word,
the soothing word, the word of confidence,
the undisturbing word, the word of praise
for sacred things like life and liberty
and the pursuit of happiness; and truth
of course, America the beautiful,
in God we trust, and in the Pentagon,
Apollo, Saturn, Jupiter, and Mars;
and Jesus saves the democratic way
of life and every day in every way
grow old along with me because the best
is surely yet to be in this fair land
possessed by people who are brave and free.

III

Like almost everyone, we want success
as measured by the instruments devised

by those who have achieved success. We want
to move into the councils of the mighty.
We know the royal things, the royal way
to royal places of security.

We're bright enough to learn the rules and play
the game and win. One exercises tact,
of course. Sequential choices must be made
discriminately, shall we say. One picks
one's schools, one's friends, profession, even spouse,
not for themselves alone but for their worth,
their calculated value, in the game.

If money is the game, don't hesitate
to take it anywhere from anyone.
But privately, select prestigious forms
of recreation with prestigious folk.
Old J. P. Morgan had a way of saying,
"You do your business thing with anyone,
your sailing only with a gentleman."

We know the game, the way to privilege.
We know the road that winds from Anathoth
up to the summit of Jerusalem;
from Anaheim to Nob Hill, San Francisco.

We understand who rules, and how and why,
and where they congregate—the royal haunts,
Mount Desert, Martha's Vineyard, Harbor Point;
the royal clubs, Bohemian and Links,
Pacific Union, Century Club, Duquesne,
Chicago, Philadelphia; and Yale,
and Stanford, Harvard, Princeton, and the rest.

We know the way to get oneself inside
the power structure of Jerusalem.
Or Babylon. And we would take the way.

IV

I, Jeremiah, want the royal way,

But there's a burning in my bones
and there's a fire in my heart
and hate is loose to tear apart
the work one loves, the love one owns.

I, Jeremiah, want the way,
But every time I draw my breath
to speak, I shout, "Destruction, death!"
And I am taken with dismay.

I could be silent like the stones
or learn to play a quieter part;
but there's a fire in my heart,
and there's a burning in my bones.

V

The burning burns, and we are driven folk,
possessed, seduced—by What, by God, by Christ,
by some infernal THOU stronger than we.
It is as if we never had the chance,
as if this burning THOU had staked her claim
not now, nor in some yesterday, nor yet
within the embryo. The seeds of burning
were planted as it were before the sperm:
"Before I formed you in the womb, I knew you!"

By God, you make us all some kind of Christ!
And that's no way to be a human being,
deprived of freedom to be free, compelled

to speak the Word they will not hear
at home in Anathoth or anywhere—
the Word of plucking up and breaking down,
the dreaded Word of violence and destruction.

VI

The burning burns inside, within my bones.
The burning Word must out. Our corporate ways
sow death. If the elite of earth cannot
desist from exploitation of the poor;
if we who *have* continue to withhold
from those who are deprived of what we have;
if those who put their highest trust in flags
cannot now own a higher loyalty;
if educated folk will not with grace
make theirs a privilege accessible
to human categories long deprived;
if in our monstrous, headless, headlong greed
we worship clever *things* our hands have made;
if we persist in making waters sick,
our air the septic tank of locomotion—
that mechanistic, technological,
swift-moving, diarrheal trafficking
on land and sea and air; if we permit
our earth, the mother of our milk and bread,
to be or to become a poison waste:
if we by lust or passion, pride or fear,
if we, by theological perversion,
permit, enhance the spread of poverty
in humankind; if we cannot at last
nurture the life of earth, subdue ourselves
and our own passions, live with peace and justice. . . .
Then, God, how burns the burning in my bones,
and I must cry of violence and destruction!

Old Jeremiah called it judgment. We,
the Jeremiahs of our present day
may call it what we will; but it is death.

The burning shut up in our weary bones;
the fire that burns internally; the Word,
the scorching Word that cannot be restrained,
is consciousness of doom—the certain sense
that if we cannot live as *human* kind,
we cannot live at all.

VII

If we could hear
as Jeremiah heard, if the raw Word
of Yahweh could break in, break through to us,
what would we hear? Suppose, let's just suppose
that vast facade, our tranquil Western front,
the heavy structure of our intellect,
were penetrated by the Word. Suppose
that hard, inhibiting, thick overlay
of conscious mind long since surrendered to
parochial notions of reality
were pierced, to leave exposed responsive depths
of mind that otherwise lie locked and frozen
beneath our stubborn surface consciousness.
Suppose we heard for once the Very Voice.
What might it say to this day's Jeremiahs?

(The setting for what follows has to be church pulpit and
pews, preacher and congregation.)

YAHWEH: Davie! You talk too much. What are you doing up
there in a black bathrobe? Who are all those people out there?
Never mind. They look very clean . . . very decent . . . very
square. Where are the beards? I always liked beards. The
prophets, you know. And of course there was my son . . .

Well, enough of this. We haven't got all day. The stubborn surface consciousness will be closing over again to become once more that hard, inhibiting, thick overlay of conscious mind—I believe those were your words. . . .

DN: Yes, Yahweh.

YAHWEH: In any case, we do not want to exceed twenty minutes for this part of the service. (*Pause*) You sometimes do, you know.

DN: Yes, Yahweh.

YAHWEH: The last time around, you pushed it very close.

DN: Yes, Yahweh. Forgive me, Yahweh.

YAHWEH: That's good. Now what are we doing today? Oh, yes. I know. Are you ready? Davie, Davie, put off-your shoes from your feet, for the place on which you are standing is holy ground . . .

DN (*interrupting*): No. Excuse me, Yahweh. That's Moses. We did the Burning Bush. We're working with Jeremiah today.

YAHWEH: You want me to begin, then—Before I formed you in the womb, I knew you.

DN: That's it.

YAHWEH: And you want the Jeremiah Word for now, in your language?

DN: Yes, Yahweh.

YAHWEH: It can be said in your very present NOW, it IS said daily in a hundred ways, but largely ignored or despised. The medium may be music, dance, satire, television, newspaper. The scene might be Eastern Europe or Southern Africa or Australia or Los Angeles. The victims of injustice might be Serbs or Croatians or South Africans or aborigines or African Americans or Korean Americans—who are also everywhere on your North American continent.

Now, are you still there, Davie?

DN: Yes, Yahweh. The important question is, Are you?

YAHWEH: I AM. I WILL BE. I CAUSE TO BE. So what you have said, and what I have said, and what we have just heard—all of this is Now-Jeremiah, or Jeremiah-Now. But there is more. You read from Jeremiah; you will know what to read:

Since the burning in old Jeremiah's bones, the fire
of burning beds and flesh, the Word
that could not be suppressed was doom AND HOPE,
and death AND LIFE; destroy and overthrow—
but also BUILD AND PLANT. Read Jeremiah:
everyone can make one's own translation.

And faith and hope and love be with you all.

VIII

Here are lines of hope from Jeremiah as written in *The New
Jerusalem Bible*. Make your own rendering into our present,
our immediate now. Make his calling and commission, and
his hope, your own.

"Come back. . . ." Yahweh declares,
"I shall frown on you no more,
since I am merciful," Yahweh declares.
"I shall not keep my anger for ever.
Only acknowledge your guilt. . . .
I shall give you shepherds after my own heart,
who will pasture you wisely and discreetly."
(Jeremiah 3:12-13*a*, 15 NJB)

"Look, the days are coming," Yahweh declares,
"when I shall sow . . . and as I once watched over [you]
to uproot, to knock down, to overthrow, destroy and
bring disaster, so now I shall watch over [you]
to build and to plant," Yahweh declares.
(Jeremiah 31:27, 28 NJB)

"You must go to all to whom I send you
and say whatever I command you. . . .

> There! I have put my words into your mouth. . . .
> to build and to plant."
> (Jeremiah 1:7, 9, 10 NJB)

It is Yahweh who speaks. And now, again, it is Jeremiah who speaks:

> "I would say to myself,
> 'I will not think about him [Yahweh],
> I will not speak in his name any more.'

> "But then there seemed to be a
> fire burning in my heart,
> imprisoned in my bones.
> The effort to restrain it wearied me,
> I could not do it."
> (Jeremiah 20:9 NJB)

IX

The burning shut up in our weary bones;
the fire that burns internally; the Word,
incendiary Word, that fights restraint
is in itself a paradox: it is
at once the anguish of our corporate drive
for death and, quite in equal strength, the sense
that we are child of God, beloved of God,
in image lacking little (but how much!)
of deity; that we are loved enough
to know that love portrayed in terms of Christ:
that we are folk, ourselves quite capable
of that same love by which we are beloved.

And given consciousness of that one Word
transcending other words, the paradox

of burning in our bones embracing dark
and light, despair and hope, will in the end
find resolution in the world's redemption
from our obsession with the ways of death.

X

Hush; listen; soft. I hear the groans
of the oppressed—life torn apart!
But there's a fire in my heart,
and there's a burning in my bones.

CHAPTER FOUR

The Burning in God and Man

Verses from Jonah and the Gospels

Jonah 1:1-3	Now the word of Yahweh came to Jonah son of Amittai, saying, "Go at once to Nineveh, that great city, and cry out against it; for their wickedness has come up before me." But Jonah . . . went down to Joppa and found a ship going to Tarshish . . . away from the presence of Yahweh.
1:4-5	But Yahweh hurled a great wind upon the sea, and such a mighty storm came upon the sea that the ship threatened to break up. Then the mariners were afraid. . . .
1:7	[And they] said to one another, "Come, let us cast lots, so that we may know on whose account this calamity has come upon us." So they cast lots, and the lot fell on Jonah.
1:11-12	Then they said to him, "What shall we do to you, that the sea may quiet down for us?" For the sea was growing more and more tempestuous. He said to them, "Pick me up and throw me into the sea; then the sea will quiet down for you; for I know it is because of me that this great storm has come upon you."
1:15	So they picked Jonah up and threw him into the sea; and the sea ceased from its raging.

1:17	But Yahweh provided a large fish to swallow up Jonah; and Jonah was in the belly of the fish three days and three nights.
2:10	Then Yahweh spoke to the fish, and it spewed Jonah out upon the dry land.
3:1-4	The word of Yahweh came to Jonah a second time, saying, "Get up, go to Nineveh, that great city, and proclaim to it the message that I tell you." So Jonah set out and went to Nineveh . . . and cried out, "Forty days more, and Nineveh shall be overthrown!"
4:5	Then Jonah went out of the city and sat down east of the city, and made a booth for himself there. He sat under it in the shade, waiting to see what would become of the city.
3:5-8	And the people of Nineveh believed God; they proclaimed a fast, and everyone, great and small, put on sackcloth. Then [the king] had a proclamation made in Nineveh: "By the decree of the king and his nobles: . . . All shall turn from their evil ways and from the violence that is in their hands.
3:9, 10 (Cf. Joel 1:13 f.)	"Who knows? God may relent and change his mind; he may turn from his [burning] anger, so that we do not perish." When God saw what they did, how they turned from their evil ways, God changed his mind about the calamity that he had said he would bring upon them; and he did not do it.
4:1-4 (Cf. Joel 2:13)	But this was very displeasing to Jonah, and he became angry [literally, was burned up]. He . . . said, "O Yahweh! Is not this what I said when I was still in my own country? That is why I fled to Tarshish at the beginning; for I knew that you are a gracious God and merciful, slow to anger, and abounding in steadfast love, and ready to relent from punishing. And now, O Yahweh, please take my life from me, for

it is better for me to die than to live." And Yahweh said, "Is it right for you to be [burned up]?"

4:6-8 [Then] Yahweh God appointed a bush, and made it come up over Jonah, to give shade over his head, to save him from his discomfort; so Jonah was very happy about the bush. But when dawn came up the next day, God appointed a worm that attacked the bush, so that it withered. When the sun rose, God prepared a sultry east wind, and the sun beat down on the head of Jonah so that he was faint and asked that he might die. He said, "It is better for me to die than to live."

4:9-11 But God said to Jonah, "Is it right for you to [burn with anger] about the bush?" And he said, "Yes, [I am burned up] enough to die." Then Yahweh said, "You are concerned about the bush, for which you did not labor and which you did not grow; it came into being in a night and perished in a night. And should I not be concerned about Nineveh, that great city, in which there are more than a hundred and twenty thousand persons who do not know their right hand from their left, and also many animals?" (RSV, "much cattle").

Mark 8:11-13 (REB) Then the Pharisees came out and began to argue with him [Jesus]. To test him they asked him for a sign from heaven. He sighed deeply and said, "Why does this generation ask for a sign? Truly I tell you: no sign shall be given to this generation." With that he left them, re-embarked, and made for the other shore.

Matthew 16:1-4 (REB) The Pharisees and Sadducees came, and to test him they asked him to show them a sign from heaven. He answered: "It is a wicked, godless generation that asks for a sign; and the only sign that will be given it is the sign of Jonah." With that he left them and went away.

Luke 11:29-30, 32 (REB)

With the crowds swarming round him he went on to say: "This is a wicked generation. It demands a sign, and the only sign that will be given it is the sign of Jonah. For just as Jonah was a sign to the Ninevites, so will the Son of Man be to this generation. . . . The men of Nineveh will appear in court when this generation is on trial, and ensure its condemnation; for they repented at the preaching of Jonah; and what is here is greater than Jonah."

Jonah 1:1-2 (paraphrase)

Now once upon a time the Word of Yahweh
confronted Jonah, son of Amittai:
"Arise and go to Nineveh, the city,
the capital of great Assyria,
and cry against it—for their wickedness
is great enough to come before my face."

I

It happened once upon a time; that is,
it never was but always is. It happens.
It happens in the way of happenings
in parables related in the Gospels;
the way of Salinger and Lewis Carroll;
the way *Of Mice and Men* and *Moby Dick*,
Wind in the Willows, *Yellow Submarine*;
the way of Ionesco, Tolkien, Milne.

The likes of Cyrus and Napoleon
are once, not once upon an any time.
But sons who spend their substance riotously,

and those who sail beneath a sea of green,
content to live in sweet oblivion;
the Holden Caulfields, Lennies, Bandersnatches,
and whales, rhinoceri, and Alices;
the Hobbits and the Toads and Pooh and Piglet—
these never were but somehow always are.

II

So once upon a very present time,
maybe today, tomorrow, yesterday,
the Word of Yahweh comes to Johnny Jonah,
the son of Amittai, or Mrs. Jones:
"Arise—this is to say, get off your stand,
your cozy status in Jerusalem,
and get yourself to Nineveh, the place,
it's any place, where life is less than life;
where hungers reign; where light is turned to dark;
where ways of death absorb the wealth and mind
of all the living.

"Go to Nineveh
the secular metropolis, the crown
at once of genius and stupidity,
the incestuous cave, colossal smog-filled space,
the putrid citadel of violence.

"Get you to Nineveh: get with it, now.
Go where the action is, depersoning,
dehumanizing action, hostile, hard.
Go where it is, the city of the world,
whose waters of compassion are polluted,
whose quality of mercy is restrained,
whose store of love long since has been depleted.

"For God's sake go to Nineveh and see—
and tell it like it is. The hour is late,
the judgment imminent, the holocaust
impending now. This is the Word of Yahweh:
My anger and frustration burn; and when
I burn, earth burns.

                    "The way to Nineveh?
It has to do not necessarily
with roads and countries, seas and continents;
it has to do with seeing, understanding;
it has to do with knowing humankind
and passionately hating everything
that robs one of one's human heritage.

"For Christ's sake, go, or come, to Nineveh!"

III

Now Johnny Jonah, listening, speaks up:
"I heard all that. Old Yahweh, how you blow!
A funny thing: you know, one possible
interpretation of your name, *Yahweh*,
connects it with a Hebrew root 'to blow.'
'The Blower' blowing over Nineveh
as if it were the bloody world gone mad.
'Tell Nineveh of judgment and proclaim
its doom,' you say. 'My anger is on fire:
the folk of Nineveh are soon to burn'—
as if your burning puts in jeopardy
the whole cock-eyed inflammable creation!"

IV

"I'll call your bluff. I'm not for Nineveh.
The people there are deaf. The die is cast
in Nineveh: the billions go to space;
to submarines and aircraft carriers;
to 'Star War' schemes; stealth bombers;
chemical and biological research for war.
The Ninevites are all enslaved
to what they call, O monstrous euphemism,
'defense'—the science and technology
of violence, destruction, and of death—
the while the weightier matters of defense,
of true defense, of justice, mercy, faith,
are tragically neglected.

                              "*I* am *not*
for Nineveh. They won't repent. Oh, sure,
they may put on a show, effect a change
of heart, pretend that they are now in fact
committed to the ways of justice, peace.
And you, Yahweh, the patient Lover-God,
loving the world enough to give your life—
this is the Gospel sense of God in Christ—
you'll simply once again give amnesty,
which is of course your way *ad nauseum.*
You will declare the judgment of your wrath—
which never would have fallen anyway—
to be suspended, utterly removed,
annulled.

"And you will talk of faith in us,
inhabitants of Nineveh. 'You care,'
you'll say to us, 'you care for objects, things,
inanimate, imperament, and as
compared to human values, human life,

without enduring worth. You are in thrall
to *things* which, so to speak, contrive to thwart
and insulate against the awful heat
of human history. While I, Yahweh,
the Holy One among you, in your midst—
I care for human life, for humankind;
I care for the renewal of creation.
With everlasting, infinite compassion,
I care for life's fulfillment!"

"Peace, Yahweh—
and by your sacred name, why pick on me?
I'd like to stay in old Jerusalem,
believing as I do that God, of course,
is packaged in the temple of our faith,
that our concerns are necessarily
identified with God's and God's with ours.
It burns me up to think that Nineveh
has any claim on Yahweh, let alone
on me. I say, to hell with Nineveh!
No Nineveh for me, in Yahweh's name!
I'm off for Tarshish. Tarshish, anyone?"

V

"Now let me tell you. Tarshish is a trip,
an absolutely never-never land—
unqualified *illusion* of escape
from Nineveh, or from Jerusalem;
the always insubstantial *fantasy*
of flight from burning God and burning flesh.
The trip is hell—it's hell to try to go
to Tarshish. God, I wish I'd headed straight
for Nineveh.

          "Three days in hell it was.
The writer Aldous Huxley penned some lines

on my unfortunate incarceration.
But he romanticized, he pietized
the whole incredible experience.
With tongue in cheek, of course, he put it so:

Seated upon the convex mount of one vast kidney,
Jonah prays, and sings his canticles and hymns,
Making the hollow vault resound God's goodness
    and mysterious ways,
Till the great fish spouts music as he swims.

"That really isn't how it is at all.
We Johnny Jonahs aren't disposed to sing
when we are caught by Yahweh in a fish
somewhere between Tarshish and Nineveh.
No one rejoices when one finds oneself
restrained from breaking loose, and brought again
to face some kind of crucifixion.

"Look at Jesus' anguish in Gethsemane."

VI

"My name is Johnny Jonah. I am one
who never was but always am—always
in search of Tarshish; always brought again
to Nineveh; and never satisfied.
If Yahweh burns in anger at the ways
of Ninevites in any Nineveh,
God cools it when a sign of hope appears.
And I, who have proclaimed God's wrath, am left
holding the bag. No wonder that I burn!

"Confound you, Yahweh, for a fickle God!
You sensitize me to the awful ways
of wicked Ninevites, and make of me
a prophet belching fire and preaching doom
on all who manufacture or contrive

devices of destruction, perpetrate
the fraudulent, support inequity,
and reinforce the old injustices.
And then, my God, you tell me in effect
that these rank people claim your hope and love.
It isn't any wonder that I burn!"

VII

So there he goes, the everlastingly
contemporary Jonah, wanting out
from Nineveh, frustrated in his flight
to Tarshish, in a manner crucified
and buried; brought again to life and light;
then mightily condemning Nineveh
for wickedness, and God for being God;
and finally in burning rage protesting
the hope and love of God for Nineveh
and saying in effect, "Burn them, not me!"

A life, a crucifixion, burial—
and then a fully human resurrection,
which nonetheless proclaims the love of God
for humankind; the openness of life
to new beginnings, fresh and new creation;
the readiness, the eagerness of God
to free us all from bondage to the past,
and set us on our way to being whole.

VIII

And here we are in our own generation.
Confronted by another life and death

and resurrection. Jesus *was*, of course,
as Jonah never was. But Jesus *is*,
as Jonah is, beyond facticity,
affirming what is true with or without
specific, literal, concrete enactment.
One who insists that Jonah's wondrous fish
and Jonah's three-day residence therein
are stuff of fact is no more off the mark
than one who wants to stake the Christian faith—
and bind all others to the test as well—
on flesh and blood and bone facticity
of the post-resurrection animation
of Jesus' body. At its best, that is
to play the role of Pharisee, to seek
a sign, to say, "Show us a miracle
and we'll believe. Make with the magic, Lord.
Defy the natural law. Give us a sign!"

But this same Jesus said with hurt and heat,
"Why does this generation ask for signs?
I tell you this: no sign is given you
except the sign of Jonah,"—which affirms,
which means, no miracle except the Word
that Yahweh cares for every "Ninevite"
(and also, even, Nineveh's "much cattle"!);
that Jonah's "resurrection" is at once
assurance to the world of "Ninevehs"
that new creation will emerge from death.

IX

The resurrection is. Unless it *is*
it never was, and if it is, it is
in faith, as from the first it was in faith.

And this is after all no Jonah. This
is Jesus Christ. This is the resurrection
of one who is at once the son of God
and child of earth.

        And if he *is* for us
then we will know that he is risen now,
that every child of earth and God may rise
up from the grave of hatred, poverty,
destruction, hunger, impotence, and war;
that death, and all the ways of making death,
will die; that God has staked the life of Christ,
the very life of God, upon the hope
of human restoration, resurrection.

Inhabitants of "Nineveh" are loved
with ultimate and everlasting love.

X

It is a time of burning, crucifixion:
It is a time of calling, resurrection.
The calling is to turning, change of heart,
repentance for our corporate ways of death.
The calling calls of human amnesty,
annulment of the past, rebirth, renewal.
It calls to everyone in "Nineveh"
that all the ways of burning, all the forms
of crucifixion may be wiped away.

The time of burning is a time of calling,
a call to sharing in the resurrection—
authentic reassurance that the ways
of death, the subtle, violent, myriad ways,

can be transformed to ways of life; and we,
this motley company of humankind
may be restored in image once again
of God who made us, and of Christ, the Word
made flesh among us—in our midst.

PART
THREE

*Word of God,
Word of Earth*

CHAPTER ONE

The Drought

(I Kings 17, author translation)

1 Elijah the Tishbite said to Ahab, "By the life of Yahweh the God of Israel whom I serve, I declare that in these immediate years there shall be neither dew nor rain but at my word."

2 Then the Word of Yahweh instructed him: "Get out of
3 here and keep heading east; hide in the Wadi Kerith at the
4 Jordan. You will be able to drink from the steam; and I have commanded the ravens to feed you there." So he put
5 into action the Word of Yahweh: he went to live in the ravine of Kerith where it approaches the Jordan; and the
6 ravens kept bringing him food, and he drank from the stream.

7 But after a while, of course, the stream petered out
8 because there had been no rain on the earth. So the Word
9 of Yahweh advised him again: "Move immediately to Zarephath, a Sidonian town, and take up your residence there. You will see: I've designated a local woman, a widow, to sustain you."

10 Accordingly, he picked up and went to Zarephath, where, coming into the town, he saw in fact a woman, a widow, gathering sticks. So he called to her and said, "Will you bring me, please, something with a little water in it, so
11 that I can drink." And as she started out to get it, he called
12 out after her, "Will you also bring me please a piece of bread." But now she responded, "I swear by the life of Yahweh your God, there is nothing baked left, but only a handful of flour in a jar and a little oil in a cruet. You just

13 found me gathering a few sticks to prepare this for my son and me to eat before we die." Elijah said to her, "Don't be afraid. Go ahead with what you propose to do; but in addition and first make out of it a small biscuit for me, and bring it to me. You may then take care of yourself

14 and your son; because this is the Word of Yahweh the God of Israel:

> The jar of flour shall not be finished
> And the cruet of oil shall remain undiminished
> 'Til the time when Yahweh again has replenished
> The face of the ground with rain."

15 She carried out the word of Elijah; and she was sus-
16 tained, she, and he, and her son, day after day. The jar of flour was not consumed, nor the cruet of oil depleted, in accord with the Word of Yahweh which was declared through Elijah.

17 Some time after all of this, it happened that the son of this woman, who was mistress of her own house, was taken ill; and his condition became so severe that he was hardly

18 able to breathe. Now she spoke to Elijah: "Why did you interfere, you man of God? You've come to me to expose

19 my own sin, and so to kill my son." "Give me your son," he said; and taking him from her arms he carried him

20 to the upper room [Elijah's own room] and put him down on the bed. Then he cried out, aloud, to Yahweh: "Yahweh, my God, can it be your intention, in addition

21a [to the drought and attendant disasters], to inflict cata-
22b strophe on the very widow who has opened her home to

23 me by killing her son?" Then he stretched himself out on the child three times with the result that he revived. Elijah picked up the child, brought him down from the

24 upper room of the house, and giving him back to his mother, he said, "See, your son lives." The woman responded, "Now I know in fact that you are of God, and that the Word of Yahweh that you speak [literally, in your mouth] is truth."

The Crisis

In significant and irreversible ways these fiercely turbulent years at the turning of centuries seem infinitely removed from the immediate past. The pace of change and its effect has been revolutionary.

The two worlds of the Cold War are gone, and the anguish and poverty and oppression in the Third World declares to all of us in our inequitable world that things will never be the same again. And with all this there is the certain knowledge among us that the years of plenty of this planet's resources are really already ended and that we must learn to live, if we will live at all, in relative drought.

Elijah's word to Ahab must now be the declaration of a permanent, if not terminal condition. The years, the centuries, the millennia of ample dew and rain of resources and of their profligate exploitation are over. The fecundity of the earth, which the Ahabs and Jezebels have always worshiped and appropriated, has been bled to barrenness. Neither Elijah's word nor even Yahweh's will restore it. This drought will endure. Of this kind of dew and rain, there shall be no more.

I do not see how contemporary discipleship, particularly on the ancient prophetic model, can be faithful either to the Word of God or the word of earth except as it is lived in a sense of critical, responsible, passionate urgency. And both these words—of God and of earth—must be heard and proclaimed simultaneously. Rubém Alves, Latin American theologian and church person, claims that "the language of the community of faith must be understood as occurring between the reading of the Bible and the reading of newspapers."[1]

Or, as a contemporary French theologian has put it, "If the Church wishes to deal with the real questions of the modern world (then) instead of using only revelation and tradition as starting points . . . it must start with facts and questions derived from history."[2]

The Word of God and the word of earth—earth as nature, as history, as humanity. In 1969, that beautiful and sensitive prophet of earth, U Thant, said that the member states of the

United Nations have a decade to solve the major problems of the world before "they have reached such staggering proportions that they will be beyond our capacity to control."[3] Was he wrong? Another earth prophet, Evelyn Hutchinson, looking not at the political, but at the ecological aspects of crisis, declared decades ago:

> Many people . . . are concluding on the basis of mounting and reasonable objective evidence that the length of life on the biosphere as an inhabitable region for organisms is to be measured in decades rather than in hundreds of millions of years. This is entirely the fault of our own species.[4]

It is the biblical creation-faith that we are charged with the responsible care of the earth. It is the Word of God that demands our hearing and responding to the word of earth. Neither nature nor history, neither history nor humanity, can longer survive, without heretofore unimaginable consequences, the sustained ruthless exploitation inflicted upon them by the powerful of the earth.

Healing: The Word and Act of the Prophet

Elijah to Ahab; prophet to king; church to its own members and to this world: In the years that are coming upon us there shall be neither dew nor rain. Conditions and terms of existence, which have obtained until now and upon which we have been accustomed to rely, will obtain no more. Drought, the crisis of alienated folk in an alienated earth, calls for radical response; and it is the sense of the text that any satisfactory resolution of crisis will result from the prophetic word, the word and act of discipleship. There shall be neither dew nor rain except at my word. The only solution lies beyond the destruction of Baal, amoral symbol of unlimited potency.

Of course this is to take liberties with the model, as is only appropriate. At the end of the next chapter, I Kings 18, Elijah effects the termination of the same drought which he proclaims in the story before us. But the living biblical word is not delivered to us in the hard rigidity of rigor mortis. It comes to us moving and alive. In the Elijah story, the life-sustaining resources recur by the action and word of discipleship—when Baal has been effectively destroyed, when the gods and goddesses of fecund, unlimited productivity are repudiated, when personal and tribal gratification are disaffirmed and Yahweh is acclaimed ultimate, whose will it is always to bring Israel out of Egypt, Philistia out of Caphtor, Syria out of Kir; to whom Judah and Ethiopia are alike; who calls for highways between the Egypts and the Assyrias of the earth; who blesses all human families, calling them all my people, the work of my hands, my heritage (see Amos 9:7 and Isaiah 19:23-25).

If we are to take these texts as suggesting authentic qualities of contemporary discipleship, we may be startled here, if not even a little disconcerted, by the measure of authority, bordering on arrogance, assumed to obtain to the prophet. There shall be neither dew nor rain except at my word, unless and until I say so. We remember that Mosaic tradition holds Moses culpable for arrogating to himself and Aaron power to produce water in the sustained drought of the wilderness. Before striking the rock from which fresh water is to gush forth, Moses cried, in long-pent-up exasperation, "Listen to me, you rebels. Must we get water out of this rock for you?" It is the harsh judgment of tradition that this indiscretion was responsible for his failure to enter the promised land (see Numbers 20:10; Exodus 17:1-7; and Psalm 106:32, 33). Our conventional piety, then, might lead us to expect another reading in the Elijah story: "There shall be neither dew nor rain except at the Word of Yahweh." We've grown accustomed to the phrase—and very comfortable with it—that God is working in history. The real worker in the Elijah stories, as for the most part in the narratives of subsequent prophets, is the prophet himself; and with uncommon emphasis in the Elijah texts, the word and the act of serving God are seen as authoritative, efficacious, and decisive—derivative, of course, of the Word of Yahweh.

It is nevertheless a matter which has obviously disturbed the traditionists, who have on occasion taken it upon themselves to "improve" the narratives according to their own taste. Elijah comes on too strong for them. In the statement that the prophet and the widow and her son were all sustained, the qualifying phrase that this was according to the word of Elijah is omitted by some Greek translators centuries later as being in improper conflict with the word of Yahweh (in vv. 5 and 16). Even some English translators eschew the phrase "the word of Elijah" and render it "she did as Elijah had said" or "had told her."

But if we take seriously the Elijah model, it may be reprimanding us for our timidity, our failure to speak and act incisively and with authority, our fear to declare the word of earth in the name of God, our disposition to say that only God can speak and act to redeem the catastrophic conditions of our human drought, the now apparently impending disaster of our exploitation of earth and humanity. If we impute any sense of revelation to these narratives, any authentic disclosure of the meaning of discipleship, then the word and act of disciple must run the risk even of appearing brash. Discipleship, ministry in the broad sense, must be effective responses to the word of earth—to be sure, in the name of God, but with the understanding that its implementation is up to us. If it is done, we will do it, to be sure in response to the Word of God and the Holy Spirit.

The first word of Elijah that we hear is a declaration of the essence of ministry, lay and professional—its foundation, its inspiration, its compulsion, its sense, its reason for being: As Yahweh the God of Israel lives . . . by the very life of Yahweh God of Israel . . . before whom I stand . . . whom I serve . . . in whose presence I live and move and have my being . . . in the name, for the sake, to the glory, toward the will, and at the call and command of Yahweh, God, Embodiment of Justice, ultimate Mother and Father of all the living, patient lover of oppressed and oppressor—by this life, which is the only Way and Truth I know, I speak what I must speak, and do what I must do!

There is always talk of the loss of the vertical in the life of the church to an alleged increasing preoccupation with horizontal concerns. But how can the Word of God and the word of earth

116

be held separate? Prophetic ministry knows neither, alone, and is able to understand the one only in immediate consciousness of the other. If one says to Elijah that he should leave matters of the drought to engineers and rainmakers, famine and poverty to the appropriate bureaucracies, human healing to the AMA, foreign affairs to Samaria/Washington, the scandals of Baal worship to the self-policing of the multinational corporations, the murderous appropriation of the little vineyards of the little Naboths around the world to the justice and the greed of the powerful, and the peace of the world to Ahab's chariots and the Pentagon—Elijah will have to say, and we in the church will have to say, we cannot do this without denying that Yahweh lives; or without removing ourselves from the presence of God.

Three scenes follow in I Kings 17, all during and in consequence of the drought. In the first, Elijah survives worsening drought and famine in the Wadi Kerith. In the second he takes up what proves to be sustaining residence with a Sidonian widow. And in the third he restores to life and health her dying son. Since all three strain the credulity of our very proper, precise, scientific, square mentality, let us suspend that inhibiting quality of mind; or, better, let us begin to abandon altogether the solid, Western, whitish, malish, prudent, reasoned stance, in which we appear to have become frozen, and, for the permanent conditions of crisis ahead of us, let us like Elijah learn to rest lightly on the earth. This means that we will say of nothing, "this is mine"; that we will regard no condition as established; that we will remain in every sense mobile; and that we will cultivate, embrace, and affirm the graces of speedy improvisation. If we are to serve now in response to Word of God and word of earth, we must be (in frame of mind if not in reality) without place, without possession, without people, without position; and insofar as we use them, we must know that they are not ours. To attempt to hold them is, if not immediately to perish, to die to servanthood. In this indefinite—I think permanent—term of crisis of the earth, the fixed base, professional, geographical, theological, ideological, with its assumption of permanence is surely ultimately an illusion.

Kerith (vv. 2-7)

Our posture in the world reminds me of lines I've had stuck in my mind since early childhood:
The boy stood on the burning deck
  Eating peanuts by the peck.
His father called; he would not go
  Because he loved the peanuts so.
Elijah leaves the place he's been. We really don't know where he came from, or even where he is when he turns eastward to be sustained by the hospitality of ravens and the diminishing flow of a brook. We meet Elijah first wherever Ahab is, and it is apparently the assumption of the narrative that everyone knows where the king is. The formal fortress/palace, built by Ahab's father, Omri, is on the summit of Samaria; but it is probable that the primary home and residence of both kings is Jezreel.[5]

The word either of God or of earth or both may tell us—Elijah is an authentic model—to go for the sake of the survival and preservation of our discipleship where, if we eat at all, it will be (what an act of trust!) at the beak of ravens. It is amusing to see what rationalists among modern commentators have proposed as alternate readings for "ravens," since that is of course a patent absurdity. By changing the vowels (which were not in fact a part of the original Hebrew text), we can read "Arabs." Or, others have argued, a case can be made, without change in the word, to "merchants." Or, according to another proposal, since the root underlying "ravens" carries the meaning "to be black," why don't we assume that Elijah was fed by blacks (by Afro-Arabians?). The rationalization is hardly better than the inference of miracle, predicating as it does Arabs or merchants or blacks coming in daily parade through the wadi, this rough, wild, godforsaken ravine, to share with Elijah the contents of their brown paper bags. Blacks feeding a white? Arabs feeding a Jew? Merchants feeding a prophet? "Ravens" is better.

An interesting aside: The Spanish Bible translates "ravens" as *los cuervos,* one meaning of which, in addition to black birds, is "corrupt priests." Let the commentators play around with that one.

A word to my colleagues "of the cloth" in formal, professional ministry. We in ordained ministry are quick to condemn our professional colleagues in medicine or law or even teaching for the abandonment of the motive of service for that of compensation. We are the ones who ought to know that the deck is burning; but our love of peanuts is not always demonstrably less than theirs. It is a cultural assumption to which we have become totally accommodated that the only reason one moves anywhere from Samaria or Jezreel is because it is a move "up" in pay and prestige.

Two or three years after we had left Stanford in the early 1970s, we returned to attend a farewell party for a medical school professor and his family we had come to know well. At table, someone spoke with regret of our having left Stanford and expressed the supposition that, even if we had wanted to stay, we could not have afforded to turn down the offer of a seminary presidency. My wife replied casually, "No, we took a cut." Now I break in to say that the deck is hot, but that I too am very fond of peanuts and have had more than my share in spite of that cut. Later in the evening, the same friend put her arm around Joy and said comfortingly and sympathetically, "I hope Davie's next move will be up."

Flour and Oil (vv. 8-16)

In the second scene of the chapter, the circumstances for the survival and promotion of the Disciple/Servant are hardly improved. The resources of amiable ravens and dying stream are to be replaced by the dubious, tenuous hospitality of an absolutely unknown and unidentified woman, a widow, and she far to the north, quite beyond the borders of Israel-Judah, in a town of Sidon through and on the other side of Queen Jezebel's home territory of Tyre. Elijah must have said, Yahweh, you've gotta be kidding!

Now we won't torture the model. Not everything fits. Where it speaks, let it speak. Where, being only itself, it cannot be also for us, then let it be, and let us be comfortable letting it be. Or take it for itself alone. Elijah comes through, if not always as a winsome guy, as fully and on the whole an admirable person, prophet, servant. He has enormous strengths, together with the whole range of qualities of unimpeachable, authentic humanity. And he and his story are blessed with an original narrator (or narrators) of equal distinction in his own calling. Despite some insensitive, overly pious, and marring accretions, we are aware that the story of Elijah is economically, simply, and brilliantly told.

There is of course absurdity in every act of faith. To live in faith in the time of our own perilous drought is to live in the assumption that if there is no bread, ravens will bring us bread; or that the widow's exhausted and nonrenewable ingredients for the preservation of life—the testimony of the word of earth—may by the Word of God and our own bold word and discipleship be made sufficient for the whole household.

> Jesus welcomed the crowds (in the thousands) and spoke to them of the kingdom of God, and cured those who had need of healing. Now the day began to wear away, and "he said to [his disciples], 'You give them something to eat.' They said, 'We have no more than five loaves and two fish. . . .' And [Jesus] said . . . 'Make them sit down in groups of about fifty each.' They did so and made them all sit down. And taking the five loaves and the two fish, he looked up to heaven, and blessed and broke them, and gave them to the disciples to set before the crowd. And all ate and were filled (Luke 9:13-17).

The widow said to Elijah (obviously in outrage and indignation), "I swear by the life of Yahweh your God, there is nothing baked left, but only a handful of flour in a jar and a little oil in a cruet . . ." But she carried out the word of Elijah; and she was sustained, she and he, and her son, day after day. The jar of flour was not consumed, nor the cruet of oil depleted, in accord with the word of Yahweh which was declared through Elijah.

I've said, Don't torture the model. Don't make rigid the process of correspondence between Elijah's ninth century B.C.E. and our twenty/twenty-first century C.E. The symbol of drought is effective and appropriate and authentic in our times—we know this; it doesn't have to be said—in ways quite beyond, but surely related to, the ecological crisis. Forms of our drought include, of course, institutionalized racism, institutionalized violence, institutionalized hypocrisy/arrogance/greed; institutionalized-nationalized-USized imperialism; institutionalized devices and procedures in operation around the world to grind the faces of the poor in the dirt and keep them there; and, by these same devices and procedures, to ensure the continued flow of wealth and the desirable goods of the world into the pockets and mouths and establishments of those who already control and possess in grotesque disproportion the produce and products of the earth.

Sickness unto Death (vv. 17-24)

This time of drought is also a time of sickness unto death. If the monumental pious declarations and postures of our past were ever justified, it cannot be now or ever again. To talk piously, superficially, glibly, and with detachment, as too often we have, of the unfolding drama of the Bible; of God who acts; of the redemption of history in God's good time; of the inevitability of the perennial presence of the poor among us, of war among us; to do so in such a way as to denigrate or disparage or depreciate the word and work and anguish of earth, the epidemic hunger and poverty and impotence that afflict like the plague most of the human family—to thus stalk across the earth in these impervious boots of a monarchical Word of God is to castrate the prophets and lobotomize Jesus Christ. We cannot now, if we ever could, afford this kind of piety, which doesn't even say, Let George do it. It says, Let God do it! Nor can we, in the midst of this vast human drought which has overtaken us, presume always to be polite to God (to say nothing of each other) and therefore to be deceiving, dissimulating. On the authority of what ancient, outmoded model do we stand only in awe before the presence of the Presence—in abject confession, in (often) self-concerned petition, in (sometimes essentially) self-seeking intercession, or in cheap, insubstantial (and it may be, illogical) thanksgiving? This is the God who wills power to the people, all God's people, all people, and not to kings and emperors and other assorted oppressors. This is the God of the poor, the oppressed, the abused, the exploited, not the god of the mighty. God knows us. We can't get by with pretension in that Presence. So, along with prayers of Thanksgiving and Confession and Intercession and Petition, let's let fly with the prayer of Protest. There is splendid precedent, authoritative example.

Here is Moses:

> Why have you treated your servant so badly? Why have I not found favor in your sight, that you lay the burden of all this people on me? Did I conceive all this people? Did I give birth to them, that you should say to me, "Carry them in your bosom, as a nurse carries a sucking child," to the land that you promised on oath to their ancestors? Where am I to get meat to give to all this people? For they come weeping to me and say, "Give us meat to eat!" I am not able to carry all this people alone, for they are too heavy for me. If this is the way you are going to treat me, put me to death at once—if I have found favor in your sight—and do not let me see my misery. (Numbers 11:11-15)

There is Job, of course, in that bitter parody of Psalm 8:

> "What are people, men and women, that you make so much of them, that you set your mind on them, visiting them every morning and testing them every moment? Will you never look away from me or leave me alone long enough for me to swallow my spit?" (Job 7:17-19, author translation)

And there is Jeremiah (rendering all the lines as address to Yahweh in a prayer of Protest):

> Yahweh, you have [deceived] me, and I was [deceived];
>   You have overpowered me, and you have prevailed.
> I have become a laughingstock all day long;
>   everyone mocks me.
> For whenever I speak, I must cry out,
>   I must shout, "Violence and destruction!"
> For [your] word has become for me

a reproach and derision all day long.
If I say, "I will not mention [you],
    or speak anymore in [your] name,"
Then within me there is something like a burning fire
    shut up in my bones;
I am weary with holding it in, and I cannot.
(Jeremiah 20:7-9)

And Habakkuk, like Jeremiah, comes very close to home:

How long, Yahweh, am I to cry for help
while you will not listen;
to cry, "Violence!" in your ear
while you will not save?

Why do you make me see wrong-doing,
why do you countenance oppression?
Plundering and violence confront me,
contention and discord flourish.

And so the law loses its grip
and justice never emerges,
since the wicked outwits the upright
and so justice comes out perverted.
(Habakkuk 1:2-4 NJB)

And so we return to Elijah and his own brief, incredulous prayer, charged with resentment and outrage if, as he fears, the little son of the widow is dead. A properly pious prayer has been added to the text, in an effort to preserve in Elijah the conventional image of the man of God; but the true and authentic word of the narrative is this: In profound exasperation and anguish of spirit, with the seemingly lifeless body of the child now lying on the prophet's own bed, Elijah cries in unmistakable meaning, "Are you really going to go through with this? As if privation of earth and people were not already enough, can you bring totally undeserved judgment on this child and on his mother by taking his life, leaving her now in consummate grief, and me in contempt and rejection? My God Yahweh!" (I Kings 17:20, paraphrased).

The child, whether dead or not, now lives. Renewed life or healing, or both, has occurred. We do not even have to bend the model: The lay and professional minister, ministry, discipleship, is acutely vulnerable to the word of earth, the human condition, as it confronts the life of ministry; and because ministry knows that the Word of God is the Word of Yahweh, God of Israel, God of the Servant, God of the Gospel. It understands that it must play its own role, speak its own word, fulfill its own function, affirm its own identity and integrity, and act its own part in responding to the Word of God and the word of earth.

Giving the child back to his mother, Elijah said, "See, your son lives." She responded, "Now I know in fact that you are of God, and that the word of Yahweh that you speak is truth."

The model is vastly simpler than our reality. But it is clear in its directive that the life of our earth is threatened as never before and that the progeny of the family of which we are a part are in critical and immediate need of healing. We have not come yet to the end of our story. The child is before us. We are called to heal, to run the risk of failing as well as the risk of succeeding. We must speak and act, toward the earth with sensitivity and compassion and courage, toward God and each other without pretense, and toward ourselves with initiative, integrity, and boldness, sensitive to the Word of God and vulnerable to the word of earth.

CHAPTER TWO

The Altars

(I Kings 18, author translation)

1   After a long while, this Word of Yahweh occurred to Elijah: You can go now to face Ahab; I'm ready to let it rain
2   over the land. So Elijah went to confront Ahab.
3   Since the famine was critical in Samaria, Ahab called in
Obadiah, his chief steward [omitting 3*b*-4 with many
5   scholars] and said to him, "Come on; we'll explore all the
sources of water and all the wadis in the land in hopes of
finding enough grass to save at least some of our horses
6   and mules and so not lose all our animals." Then dividing
the land between them for their search, Ahab went one
way, and Obadiah took the other way by himself.
7   Now, while Obadiah was on his way, whom should he
encounter but Elijah; and recognizing him, he fell on his
8   face. Then he said, "So it is really you, my Lord Elijah?"
9   He answered, "It is! Go say to your master, 'I've just seen
Elijah!'" But Obadiah countered, "What have you got
10   against me, that you consign this servant of yours to death
at Ahab's hand? By the life of Yahweh your God, the
nation or kingdom doesn't exist to which my master hasn't
already sent to apprehend you; and when they answered,
'He isn't here,' he demanded a formal declaration from
11   that kingdom or nation that you were not to be found. And
12   you're telling me to go say to my master, 'I've just
seen Elijah!' What will happen? As soon as I leave you, the
Spirit of Yahweh will whisk you away I know not where; I
will go in to report to Ahab; and when he can't find you,
13   he will kill me—and I, your servant, I've been from child-

125

hood on a Yahweh worshiper! Has no one told you, my Lord, what I did when Jezebel slaughtered the prophets of

14 Yahweh; that I hid a hundred of the Yahweh prophets in caves, by fifties, and kept them supplied with food and

15 drink? And now you command me to announce to my master that Elijah is here! He will kill me!" Elijah replied. "I swear by the life of Yahweh of hosts whom I serve [to whom I am committed or in whose presence I live] that I will confront him this very day."

16 Obadiah then left to intercept Ahab; and when he broke

17 the news to him, Ahab went to meet Elijah. As soon as Ahab saw Elijah, Ahab said to him, "Is it [really] you, you

18 troubler of Israel?" Elijah answered, "I'm not the one

19a who's troubled Israel, but you and your father's entourage. Now will you convene all Israel for me at

20 Mount Carmel." So Ahab sent a summons throughout

21 Israel and brought all of the people together on Mount Carmel. Elijah stood and addressed them all: "How long will you go on vacillating between the two alternatives? If Yahweh is God, follow him; or if Baal, follow him." The

22 people answered him not a word. Again Elijah addressed the people: "I myself am the only prophet of Yahweh left;

23a but the prophets of Baal number four hundred fifty. Now

25a let us have two bulls" [23a]. Then to the prophets of Baal, Elijah said, "You all choose one of the bulls and prepare it

23c first, because there are a lot of you [25a]; and I will myself

24 prepare the other bull [23c]. You pray aloud in the name of your God as I will do in the name of Yahweh; and it shall be that the God who responds with fire, he is God." To which all the people responded with a shout of approval [24].

26 Accordingly, they [the prophets of Baal] took the bull, prepared the sacrifice, and from morning until noon they

27 prayed in the name of Baal, shouting, "O Baal, answer us!" But there was no sound, nor any response. Now they performed their limping dance around the altar they had made; until at noon Elijah called out, taunting them, "Cry

28 louder, for he is a god: maybe he's meditating; or he's

gone to the john; or he's off on a trip; or perhaps he's asleep and needs to be waked up." Crying louder and
29 louder, and in conformity with their tradition, they gashed themselves with swords and spears until they were bleed-
30 ing profusely. Even with the passing of midday, they continued in prophetic ecstasy; but there was no voice, there was no answer, there was no sign of attention. Then Elijah
33 said to all the people, "Come in closer toward me"; and they all moved in toward him. He rebuilt the [old] Yahweh
37 altar which was in ruins [omitting vv. 31-32], laid the wood [for the fire], carved the bull and placed it on the wood. Then he said [omitting to v. 37], "Answer me, Yahweh, answer me, so that this people may know that you,
39 Yahweh, are God, and that as you let them go from you, it
40 is yours also to bring them back."[1] Then the fire of Yahweh struck [omitting the balance of v. 38], and when the people saw it, they fell, prone, and then cried, "Yahweh, he is God; Yahweh, he is God!"[2] Elijah said to the people, "Seize the prophets of Baal; let none of them escape." They seized them; and Elijah led them down to the Wadi Kishon and slaughtered them there.[3]
41 Now Elijah said to Ahab, "Get moving; eat and drink;
42 because there is the sound of the swish of rain." So Ahab went to eat and drink; but as for Elijah, he climbed up to the top of Carmel and crouched down on the ground with
43 his face between his knees. He said to his servant, "Go over there, now; look out to sea." He went and looked:
44 "There is nothing at all," he said. Seven times Elijah asked him to go back; and in fact the seventh time, he reported, "Yes—I can see a cloud no bigger than [one's] hand rising
45 up out of the sea." Elijah said, "Go tell Ahab, 'Harness your chariot and get going, before the rain stops you.' "
46 Even as this was taking place, the skies grew dark with clouds, the wind came, and then heavy rain. Ahab mounted his chariot and made for Jezreel; and with [as it were] the hand of Yahweh upon him, Elijah pulled himself together [4] and went, as runner to the chariot, all the way to Jezreel.

The Continuing Crisis

The fundamental and perennial circumstance of crisis has always obtained for a majority of the people of earth, although many of them, living tenuously, perilously, miserably, vulnerably, have been innocent of a sense of crisis. If in all ages some have believed themselves to be, or have in fact been, on relatively secure and durable plateaus; if, as appears to be the case, some of our present companions of earth regard the conditions of their life as being thus established and unassailable, such an assessment is now patently naive. The crisis of the relatively secure of the earth is made the more critical by their real, or it may well be feigned, complacency. One wonders whether apparently confident, comfortable, successful church persons are, in the depth of their being, as certain of the durability and righteous justification of their status of relative vast privilege in the world as appearances are contrived to suggest. Is the sociologist-critic of the church describing the real thing or a masquerade of both people and preacher when he writes, "It is as if there had been no Sermon on the Mount. . . . Sunday will remain the same: the American silent majority sitting righteously in the pews listening to silent sermons."[5] Pretended complacency, if that is what it is, is profoundly sick and makes the condition of crisis the more insidious.

But it is much more than this, isn't it? We, among the privileged of earth, have appropriated and exploited the earth and all that is in it, the world and those who dwell therein; we have founded our folly now not only upon the seas but as well in space; and we have established the ineradicable marks of our vandalism over the virginal, variegated, speechless faces of the earth and, by the billions, on the innocent and until now largely submissive faces of the human family.

Who is we? All of us together of the earth are pushing in number toward six billion. But we who have our way in the earth are a dwindling minority of the total, living mainly in North America, Western and Eastern Europe, and Japan. We consume the lion's share of the world's energy and most of the other mineral wealth of the earth. The rest of the world's population gets by on what we do not use—or what we discard.

And this too, of course, heightens and intensifies the very critical tensions of our time with which, for an indefinite future, we shall have to live. From among our own oppressed in North America and Europe, as well as from the Third World continents of Latin America, Asia, and Africa, eloquent voices, many from our own ranks of church and ministry, are telling us, the privileged minority, that these conditions of gross inequity and imbalance may not and will not endure. Innocence of the ghastly conditions of their particular human crisis—grinding poverty, economic slavery, disease; malnutrition that stunts the development of the brain and maims intelligence; thwarted, inhibited stature, physical and psychological; shockingly premature death—innocence of this awful truth is at a furious pace giving way to a new consciousness and conscience, to conscientization. The day of the sustained maintenance of the conditions of the comfortable, secure, developed plateau are over.

> The poor countries are becoming ever more clearly aware that their underdevelopment is only the by-product of the development of other countries. . . . Moreover, they are realizing that their own development will come about only with a struggle to break the domination of the rich countries. . . . A broad and deep aspiration for liberation inflames the history of mankind in our day, liberation from all that limits or keeps man from self-fulfillment, liberation from all impediments to the exercise of his freedom.[6]

Part of the definition of our own condition of crisis—crisis USA—lies precisely here. If we say to Father Gutiérrez, "Power to your revolution; power to your people," he will respond, as he has, that "there can be authentic development for Latin America only if there is liberation from the domination exercised by the great capitalist countries, and especially by the most powerful, the United States of America."[7]

It is most emphatically not my intention to suggest solutions for these overwhelming problems of earth out of the ancient narratives about Elijah, as remarkable a creation as he and they are. But what meager stuff we have on that ministry puts it consistently in a context of crisis as severe for its ninth-century

B.C.E. setting as ours in these years between centuries as it were. How does the consciousness of crisis affect our North American ministry and discipleship, which, quite apparently up to the present, have been conducted in and on the plateau?

Now the famine was critical in Samaria; the crisis was severe.

The text before us, I Kings 18, begins with the promise of rain and ends in fact with the relief of the drought. The three sections of the chapter deal centrally, successively, and brilliantly with three persons, two altars, and one priest.

Three Persons (vv. 2b-19)

In the preceding chapter we remarked on the narrator's skill in conveying character and personality in the response of person to situation and of person to person. The first section of this chapter is in three brief scenes in which persons, simply and wholly as persons, respond under consciousness of urgency to the critical situation and/or to each other.

Ahab and Obadiah (vv. 2b-6)

The famine was critical in Samaria; the crisis was severe. King and First Chancellor, President and Chief of Staff as it were, or, in the ecclesiastical establishment, Minister (or, you should excuse the expression, Senior Minister) and Chairperson of the Board or the congregation themselves and in person take on work deemed under the old "normal" conditions of life on the plateau to be the appropriate task of lesser persons, persons of lower rank or, as we have always preferred to say, persons who do not have to bear the heavy responsibilities that are ours.

Some scholars would insist that this notice has to be a piece of pure legend. How naive, they would argue, to represent the king and his highest-ranking minister out looking for feed for the horses themselves, since the historical Ahab certainly had lower-ranking staff for such a task! But this is Israel, not Phoenicia; the United States, not some fascist state; this is the people of Yahweh, not the people of Baal; this is the Church, not the State. And it is drought in Israel, where horses, and no doubt people, are dying; as it is crisis in our land and on our earth, where people, good people, innocent people, in appalling numbers and proportions, are hope-less and, in essence, life-less.

If it was legitimate on the plateau to pull ministerial rank, or to preach and live as if there existed a kind of clean Christian rank for all of us in the church, we know now that this may not be in Israel in drought, in the church-in-the-world under conditions of sustained exigency. The Word of God and the word of earth are met in us, and we are left without rank. We go ourselves in search of green grass and of such means as may alleviate the ravages of an earth whose prevalent systems are advantageous for so few and demeaning and destructive for so many.

And we will have our own critics who will tell us that this is naive and childish; that in real history it will always be given to some to live with death and to us, by the grace and calling of God, to live. But what of Yahweh, what of Christ—in whose presence we exist? What of the biblical faith in which we stand? What of the Word of God and the word of earth—which is the Word of the Cross? Whatever the past, ministry, discipleship now demands that we ourselves take to the dirty, dangerous roads on behalf of life that is in jeopardy.

We will find Elijah there.

Obadiah and Elijah (vv. 7-15)

Shift identification now in the second scene. It is Obadiah and Elijah. It is church members and prophetic Word. And God be praised that in the midst of crisis and even the near presence of death, there is place for playful imagination, for humor, for laughter, for caricature, for irreverence, for wild hyperbole—and in all of this, and because of it all, an implicit display of human affection. If on that hard, irrecoverable ground of facticity somewhere underlying the story, the historical Elijah heard such a marvelously creative, whimsical outburst from the historical Obadiah, then Elijah must have laughed aloud before he reassured Obadiah with an oath that he would by God face the king that day! Of course if the narrator had originally informed us of Elijah's pleasure and amusement in Obadiah's superbly comic performance, subsequent traditionists would have removed the notice as out of keeping with the proper character of a proper prophet. In any case it would not have survived down to this day. Some years ago at Yale I introduced to a visiting European biblical scholar one of my own Ph.D. students who was writing a dissertation on humor in the Old Testament. When I said this to my distinguished colleague, he froze in horror and said indignantly, "What humor?"

In our own expression of ministry as we are living it, as we will live it, we will laugh and let laugh. And to my ordained colleagues I say, since it is in God's presence that we exist or, more literally, before whose face we are standing, there is no essential difference in our stance before an Obadiah or before the altar; and quite deliberately I seize this moment of the text to urge that in preaching and in the conduct of public worship, laughter be permitted, encouraged, elicited. Every one of us in the business of "professional" ministry knows the occasional inevitable liturgical goof. God is better praised by our capitalizing on it than by the pious attempt to gloss it over. Not all, but most sermons miss the chance to strike a blow for "the kingdom" that do not at some point hold up for general laughter some quality of the familiar common life of our time and place.

I'm saying of humor, love it, cherish it, cultivate it, even and especially when you yourself are the quality upheld. The Elijahs and Obadiahs both are better able to live with each other, and particularly under straitened circumstances, when laughter is a constant companion of total ministry.

Elijah and Ahab (vv. 16-19)

Here it is Elijah and Ahab: prophet and king; minister/servant/disciple and establishment—or structure, or system, or institution; or church and state. Let me reiterate the authenticity, the authority, of the Elijah model. In the traditions of Judaism he is ranked second only to Moses. The impression that he made on his contemporaries and on succeeding generations down to the Christian era and beyond is eloquently attested, of course, in the narratives that we are addressing; in the stories and legends about him in II Kings (1 and 2) and II Chronicles (21:12ff.); in the remarkable word of Malachi (4:5f.) that before the "great and terrible" Day of Yahweh, Elijah will come to heal the alienation between parents and children; in the praise heaped on him by Ben Sirach in Ecclesiasticus (48:1-11); in repeated references reflecting unsurpassed esteem in apocalyptic tradition (e.g., Revelation 11:3ff.) and in the Gospels where, among other tributes, Elijah, Moses, and Christ are the three transfigured images on the Mount (Matthew 17, Mark 9, Luke 9); of course also in Talmudic and Midrashic sources; and in the fact of Elijah's annual dramatic "reappearance" during Judaism's celebration of the Seder.

In broad-ranging, informed consensus, he is not so much the last of the preclassical prophets as he is the first of that phenomenal succession which continues, then, in the next century in Amos, Hosea, Micah, and Isaiah. Hermann Gunkel, in a sense the unique parent of us all in modern scholarship, despite his insistence on legend's supervision of the Elijah narratives as we receive them, nevertheless affirms on the one hand Elijah's kinship with the greatest of all ministers of ancient Israel, Moses, in their mutual contention with their own people; and, on the other hand, Elijah's legitimate and immediate relationship to the great prophets who follow him and who, essentially, continue the work he began.[8]

The precise phrase that Ahab uses in greeting Elijah does not occur again in subsequent prophetic narratives, but the sense of it conveys the consistent, prevailing annoyance, irritation, frustration, anger, or hostility of king and people—can we say politicians and middle Israelites?—toward the prophet (or the prophetic church): "You troubler of Israel, you!"

In such a matter as this, it may be that no one may call the terms for another, no ministering person for any other, no citing of attributes for ministry in general from one's own assessment of general ministry. But you will let me speak personally and say that I do not see how ministry that presumes to honor the prophetic model, as at least in part determinative of the role, can be fulfilled without drawing intermittently but persistently the same essential charge. The worship of Baal, in middle

Israel or in middle America (we should say middle USA), is rampant. It is what Paul called the exchange of "the glory of immortal God for an imaged shape like mortal man" (Romans 1:23 REB). In this world, in this time, in ministry responsive to the Word of God and the word of earth; in a nation and a popular church in which it is as if there were no Sermon on the Mount; in such a time of durable earth crisis, we of the prophetic model will not only be *called* troublers of Israel, we will *be* in Ahab's sense, troublers of Israel.

And we of the faith will have to have the courage to do what Elijah did, that is, fling the epithet back in the accusers' teeth:[9] It is not I who have troubled Israel, but you and your family's entourage, you and your kind, you and your acquisitive systems. It was not the draft-and-war resisters who were troublers of Israel, but you the guardians of structures of racism, of imperialism, of exploitation. It is not Cesar Chavez and his union that have troubled Israel, but you and your devices of callousness and greed which hold in subhuman servitude the life of farm-working Chicano families from young to old. It is not militant blacks; it is not aggrieved, bitter Native Americans; it is not a newly assertive breed of women; it is not still sometimes viciously persecuted gays and lesbians; it is not the alienated, intellectual radical left who are troublers of these states of ours, but us, USA, we, all of us of relative power, who let the dream for all of us become a nightmare for all of them. Prophet/Minister/Disciple to people and nation: Not I (or maybe even I?) but you and your inherited ways are troublers of the earth.

A great contemporary Elijah, Archbishop Dom Helder Camara, then of Recife, Brazil, urged on us all the creation of "a world that is more breathable."[10] It is not he, or the vast majority of Brazilians, but a few of them, in part under demonic USA tutelage, that create and preserve there and similarly in other parts of the earth the nonbreathable world, the miserable conditions of human suffocation.

Three persons; Ahab, Obadiah, Elijah. Ahab to Obadiah: We'll do it ourselves. Obadiah to Elijah: You're a spook, buddy! Elijah to Ahab: Troubler of Israel—not I, but you. Word of God, word of earth. Prophetic Ministry—to both.

Two Altars (vv. 20-40)

In the center of this scene stand two altars, one of Yahweh, one of Baal.[11] The issue of the Carmel convocation is drawn, not by the desertion of one for the other, not by the defection of Yahwists to Baalism, but by the widely held assumption in Yahwist Israel that Yahwism may also embrace Baalism and that one may worship at the Baal altar and at the same time remain Yahwist. In the course of the scene Elijah repairs the Yahweh altar (the primary sense of the Hebrew verb here is that he "healed" the altar) which had been ruined—we can only guess—perhaps by an act of religious vandalism, or by neglect, or indeed immediately in the course of the frenetic, violent performance of the Baal prophets. Elijah understands that the two altars may not stand in the same sanctuary and that the Baal altar may not be honored without tacit denial of Yahweh and prostitution of the Yahweh faith. His own prophetic passion comes to a boil over the accommodation of Yahwism to Baalism. How long will you go on believing that you can be Yahwist when you are also Baalist?

Professor von Rad comments on the scene:

> It must have come as a great surprise to [the Carmel Convocation] that Elijah viewed the matter as a case of "either-or." At the time no one else saw as he did that there was no possibility of accommodation between the worship of Baal and Israel's ancient Yahwistic traditions. . . . [For Elijah] the co-existence, or rather the coalescence, of the two forms of worship, in which the rest of the people were perfectly at home, was intolerable.[12]

"Coalescence" is a good word for it. Elijah's address to the Carmel assembly begins with a question, enigmatic in the Hebrew, which I have translated, "How long will you go on vacillating between the two alternatives (that is Yahweh and Baal)?"[13]

The New Revised Standard Version reads: "How long will you go limping with two different opinions?"

The New Jerusalem Bible: "How long do you mean to hobble first on one leg then on the other?"

The Revised English Bible: "How long will you sit on the fence?"

Montgomery's Commentary on Kings (ICC): "How long are you hobbling . . . at the two forks [of the road]. i.e., hopping now on one leg, now on the other, before the dilemma. . . . Elijah is here using some popular phrase."[14]

And Skinner's commentary: "The literal sense of the Hebrew is obscure, but the idea of the question is clear from what immediately follows. It satirizes the attempt to combine two religions so incongruous as those of Baal and Yahweh."[15]

However rendered, this is the perennial prophetic question which was and still must be addressed unceasingly to the institutionalized manifestations of the biblical faith whose easy coalescence with Baal worship takes place whenever and wherever that faith becomes provincialized, parochialized, and accommodated to the culture in such a way that the adherents lose altogether the sense of critical distinction between Yahweh and Baal, between the Word of God and the word of persons, between the word of earth and the word of the system, between God who is and god who is fashioned, God who creates and god who is created—in sum, between God and his cultural image or, more bluntly, between Christ and mammon. Jesus said, "You cannot serve both," knowing full well that this was precisely the prevailing religious situation of his own people. He spoke prophetically (see Matthew 6:24).

In her series of essays entitled *Liberation Theology*, Rosemary Ruether cites in several contexts the fourth-century alliance, mutually beneficent in certain respects, between Constantinian Rome and Palestinian Christianity. She writes that it is

> the ambiguity [How long will you vacillate between the two alternatives] and tragedy of Christianity [that] a faith with roots in revolutionary messianic hope . . . was co-opted into the imperialist ideology and social structure of the later Roman empire . . . Christianity itself was used to sanctify and perpetuate the hierarchical society and world view of classical culture.[16]

For the church it was of course a kind of alliance which has been repeated and reinforced down to this moment. This ambiguity and tragedy in all the institutional expressions of biblical faith may be in some measure always and inevitably present. The process of coalescence, of accommodation, of succumbing to co-optation is to some degree continuous, and it must be therefore continuously exposed, challenged, and checked. This is the essence of prophetic ministry, a ministry never done, never completed.

This process, this working tendency toward the coalescence of Yahweh and Baal, can be observed in almost any church in this country, in almost any pulpit, in almost any pew. We will not agree, perhaps, as to where or in whom a patently co-opted faith, an ambiguous Christianity, appears most conspicuously, most tragically; but many of us are painfully aware of it in some of the most popular, widely heard, sometimes lionized clergy of our time. I think it is true of them and their hearers, as apparently it was in the Israel of Elijah and Ahab, that they really do not know the extent to which their Word of God has been twisted, tortured, adulterated by its possibly innocent and unconscious fusion with the word of decent, respectable, prosperous, prevailing white, capitalist, North American woman and man. The biblical faith, with roots in revolutionary messianic hope, which is itself rooted in the prophetism of ancient Israel/Judah, is even now, and daily, used to sanctify and perpetuate the life, culture, security, and privilege not now of imperialist Rome, but of the imperialist United States.

Is it possible that the presence of the flag of the United States of America in the sanctuary of the church signifies the coalescence of Yahweh and Baal, of Christ and culture? In other settings that flag may represent our best and highest national achievements and aspirations. But I can't escape the feeling that in the church, the national flag betrays again the ambiguity and tragedy of contemporary biblical faith, rooted in revolutionary messianic hope but, alas, comfortably accommodated to the self-seeking ways of an inevitably corrupted temporal state.

From time to time I have had to address the vastly overworked, unresolved, often heatedly controverted subject of the relationship of the seminary to the church. Some in the churches tend to believe that the seminaries are hopelessly detached from the realities of the workaday world and that seminary graduates are rendered in fact maladroit if not down-right incompetent by the very training designed to fit them for ministry. They become fit, if they do at all, only when prudent, mature lay and other clergy minds already in the church prevail over them, and when the hard realities of the church in this particular capitalist society are beaten into them. Precisely.

On the whole, I'm optimistic about the increasing détente between church and seminary and, at the same time, over the mutual creativity and productivity of the inevitably continuing tension in their intimate, indispensable relationship. As a consummately biblically oriented observer, I remain unalterably persuaded of one requisite quality in the relationship. The seminary must remain in some sense prophet to the church. The one thing the seminary may not do is send out into the church clergy who do not know the difference between the two altars and who, in the language of the model, bless the altar of Baal in the name of Yahweh, or the enterprises of the system in the name of Jesus Christ. The seminary must purify itself and the church against the unceasing incursions of Baal. But it would be oversimplification if not institutional idolatry to suggest that the seminary play in fact the very role of Elijah to the contemporary church of the two altars. God knows the seminary has its own dual or multiple altars to work through and around. I can tell you that among my moments of greatest frustration and discouragement have been on those recurrent June days when as a seminary president I handed an M.Div. diploma to a young, bright graduate who had nevertheless survived four years of college and three years of seminary unemancipated from the prevailing cultural slavery, unawakened to the word of anguished earth, indiscriminate between the Word of God and the word of the nation, undisturbed by, or even unaware of, the urgency of prophetism, and apparently innocent of the radical and loving, ruthless and merciful, devastating and redeeming claim of the Gospel upon us. That claim is Elijah to all of us in the church: "How long will you go on in this egregious fusion of Yahweh and Baal?" How long, how long?

We in biblical discipleship tend to be awed by the structures and potency of the establishment of Baal, even though we know, somewhere down there in the timid, secret resources of faith, that all the stuff of Baal doesn't make God—power, technological sophistication, machismo, sex, political, military, and economic domination, energy independence (ha!). Out of Baal, even at high noon (which is right now) with all his desperate, violent prophets screaming around his altar—out of Baal we really know, don't we, that there will be no sound, no response; no voice, no answer, nor even any sign of attention. The fire that lights the sacrifice and kindles worship, and the Word that creates, judges, and redeems, is not there.

In the Elijah model, part of the work of prophetic ministry is the courageous, authentic appropriation and imposition of the taunt of Elijah (v. 27) upon ourselves and upon the whole church. It is the staid, very scholarly, very proper *International Critical Commentary* that best describes it. "Elijah's satire in a nutshell is the raciest comment ever made on Pagan mythology."[17] Here too is high, if off-color, satirical humor in the Elijah stories, this time from Elijah himself. Sure Baal is God; a meditating, trip-taking, sleeping-waking, and—in the midst of all that, dropped as it were casually—toilet-going God! Pagan mythology it is, ensconced in our time and embraced in our churches, where we have supposed that we can know the glory of immortal God while worshiping also at the altar of our powerful and overwhelmingly impressive national Baal, an image, in the final analysis, simply made by human minds and hands.

In a first draft of this chapter, before I really worked this section freshly through again, I concluded the discussion of the text of I Kings 18:20-40 with this conventionally pious comment:

> I reject vehemently, [I wrote] and out of hand the last verse of this section (v. 40): "Elijah said to the people, 'Seize the prophets of Baal; let none of them escape.' They seized them; and Elijah led them down to the Wadi Kishon and slaughtered them there." [Then I went on to say] I quite understand the ancient, binding custom of what is called the "ban" by the imposition of which, as the New Jerusalem Bible apologetically footnotes, "in this war between Yahweh and Baal those who serve Baal suffer the fate of the conquered in the warfare of the times." But [I said in this earlier draft] it is an utterly time-bound notice, and its value in the text is, for us, sharply negative.

I take it back now. I took it back. Again, I cannot presume to make for anyone else the precise contemporary interpretation of the notice of the slaughter of the Baal prophets; but this awful scene, whatever the facts underlying it, is absolutely coherent with and essential to what has gone before. Elijah denies us the course of courteous rapprochement by which, the sermon preached, the Word spoken (as we believe and hope), the "victory" won, we shake hands all around—and continue to live with the two altars. That's what disciples and prophets and ministers and priests in the biblical faith—with all too uncommon exception—have been doing for thousands of years.

If now Elijah's drought of the moment ends, our essential situation of crisis appears to be continuous in our future. A radical break is called for, a radical separation of the two altars and a radical renewal of the biblical faith. In and of themselves, these lines of slaughter are horrible. We do not want to hear them or translate them or, in whatever way appropriate to our own time and ethic, act upon them. But there it is, and it is a "true" word, if we "translate" it sensitively. "Elijah said to the people, 'Seize the prophets of Baal; let none of them escape.' They seized them; and Elijah led them down to the Wadi Kishon and slaughtered them there."

God grant that no one reading this take me to be condoning for our own time any such violence, to say nothing of slaughter. The sense of the model for us is the urgency of the imperative: Break, totally and radically, with Baal!

One Priest (vv. 41-46)

> I think one cannot find in Hebrew prose
> A passage more poetically conceived
> And executed. In its choice of words
> As in its structure, it is unsurpassed.

Elijah said to Ahab, "Stir yourself,
Take food and drink; because I hear the swish
Of rain." So Ahab went to eat and drink.
But not Elijah; climbing to the top
Of Carmel, crouching on the ground with face
Between his knees, he asked his servant, "Now
Go out and look across the sea." He went.
"But there is nothing there at all," he said;
So, seven times Elijah sent him back.
The seventh time the servant said, "Yes sir!
I see a cloud no bigger than a hand
Arising from the sea." Elijah said,
"Go quick, tell Ahab, 'Harness up and move,
Before the rain prevents you!' "

All the while
The skies grew dark with clouds, the wind arose—
Then heavy rain. Mounting his chariot,
The king made for Jezreel. By Yahweh's might
The prophet pulled himself together; and,
As runner to the chariot, he went
With Ahab all the way to Jezreel's gate.

We of the church of Jesus Christ are one—
One prophet/servant/minister—or priest:
The priesthood of believers, priests to all.

What does this say to all of us disciples,
In crisis now sustained and durable?
What now of servanthood for those of us
Within the "better" churches of the land?
What now of ministry to "royalty,"
To those who eat and drink and ride about
In mighty chariots; who know no hurt
Though drought and famine stalk the earth
And decimate the human family;
Who do not know, or will not face the fact,
That their secure existence is maintained
At frightful cost to all the dispossessed?

How, minister to "royalty," who call
The prophets troublers of the church,
Disturbers of the Christian peace, meddlers
In matters—so they say—irrelevant
To life in faith and hope and love; for whom
The double altar is imperative;
Who seek to shape the deity in form
That sanctifies the "royal" of the earth?

What then of ministry to "royalty"—
Since quite precisely it is these to whom
We minister? Indeed, we have to say,
We've met the royalty and they are us!

Disciple/minister is one—one priest
Who must be prophet/Servant/priest to all.
Elijah does not cut himself adrift
From them; he does not cry a plague on them
And on their entourage—not yet at least.
One commentator notes Elijah's courtesy
"In bidding monarch to refresh himself."[18]
But while it is the wont of "royalty"
To eat and drink, the prophet/minister,
Close to the word of earth and sensitive
To Word of God, searches and waits for sign
And way of blessing of the families
Of earth, of sweet relief from poverty,
Injustice, and oppression—from the drought
Of inhumanity and misery.

The prophet/minister is one—one priest
Who must be minister and priest to all.
We minister among the "royalty."
We serve the Word of God and word of earth.
Numbered among oppressors, in the main,
Are our constituents, whom we must hold
In love and understanding, though we know
The "royal" ways.

We do not enter, then,
Their chariots, but run somehow along,
In touch with them, beside them, holding on.
By Yahweh's might, his hand on us, we keep
Our own integrity and work to see
The single Yahweh altar in the church.

Disciples have a priesthood to fulfill:
We must be minister and priest to all.

CHAPTER THREE

The Cave

(*I Kings 19*)

Virtually all modern scholars in all the surviving biblical faiths (except, of course, those of essentially fundamentalist persuasion) are agreed that the four primary Elijah narratives (I Kings 17–19, 21) have suffered intrusion, alteration, and expansion in the long centuries of transmission before they became unalterably fixed in the early years of our own Common Era.

Here is the narrative of the Cave (I Kings 19) as it may first have come to form, oral or written, still in Elijah's own century. The reading is reconstructed from the present Hebrew text in consultation with other primary versions and translations, and out of respect for the critical judgments of major scholars of the twentieth century. At the same time, I hope it is not necessary for me to say I do not believe that this or any other comparable effort may lay claim to the precisely literal recovery of the text as it was first given determinative form by the genius of the original Elijah narrator(s). This, one knows, is an achievement that may never be.

It is, however, clear that the story is now disfigured, not only by would-be "improvers" of the textual tradition but also by an indiscriminate fusion in the popular mind of the Elijah and Elisha images and narratives. One has only to compare the two literary parallels (there are no more) in the two cycles of stories—those of the flour and oil, and of the widow's son—to be aware of the historical and conceptual chasm that separates them. The Elisha parallels are a rank and, of course, insubstantial imitation—one has to say, again in quotes, "improvement"—of the Elijah episodes, designed to represent Elisha as the greater miracle worker. Indeed, even subsequent Elijah tra-

144

ditionists have touched the narratives here and there so as to say to the rival Elisha people, "But you see, our prophet too was quite a miracle worker!"

In the four chapters of 1 Kings that are in the main the creation of the Elijah narrator, we meet a highly gifted verbalist, who is given to the use of unique words, forms, and structures; who is relatively sophisticated; who, as compared with the Elisha narrators, for example, appears to be notably disinterested in miracle for the sake of miracle; and who shares with Elijah himself a kind of precognition of the substance of classical prophetism.

His work ranks with the finest classical Hebrew prose to be found anywhere in the Old Testament, displaying a phenomenal verbal/literary technique in the use of humor and irony, in subtle, sensitive character portrayal, and in effective, varied appeal to human emotion. And in the reconstruction and/or creation of dialogue, the Elijah narrator is unsurpassed.

Here, then, a critical reconstruction of the narrative of the Cave.

On the Way to the Cave: I Kings 19:2-6a, 8

2 Now Jezebel sent this word to Elijah: "If you are Elijah, I
3 am Jezebel!" Frightened for his life, he ran away; and when he got to Beersheba in Judah, he left his servant
4 there and went on himself for a day into the wilderness; until at last he sat down under a broom tree and prayed that he might die. "I've had it, Yahweh," he said. "Take
5 my life: I'm no better than those who have gone before me." He lay down there and went to sleep; until suddenly
6a someone touched him and said, "Wake up and eat." He
8 looked about—and there at his head was a stone-baked biscuit and a jar of water. So he ate and drank and then, on the strength of that nourishment, he went on to Horeb.

The Stay at the Cave:
I Kings 19:9a, 11b, 12-15, 18

9a   Coming there to a cave, he spent the night.
11b And there was a mighty wind
     Not in the wind was Yahweh
     And after the wind, earthquake
     Not in the earthquake was Yahweh
12   And after the earthquake, fire
     Not in the fire was Yahweh
     And after the fire—
     A sound of gentle silence.
13   Upon hearing this, Elijah covered his face with his robe
     and went out to take his position at the mouth of the cave.
     It was only now that the Word of Yahweh was: "What are
14   you doing here, Elijah?" Elijah replied: "I have been pas-
     sionately devoted to Yahweh, God of hosts, even while the
     people of Israel have abandoned you. Your altars they
     have destroyed, your prophets they have put to death
15a with the sword. I am left now, myself, alone; and they are
     after me to take my life!" But Yahweh answered him, "Go
18   back the way you have come; because there are still seven
     thousand left in Israel whose knees have never bent to
     Baal, nor whose lips have kissed him!"

The Way Back from the Cave:
I Kings 19:19-21

19   Leaving that place [Elijah] came upon Elisha son of
     Shaphat plowing with twelve yoke of oxen in front of him,
     and he with the twelfth. As Elijah passed by, he tossed his
20   robe over him. Leaving the oxen, [Elisha] ran after Elijah
     and said, "Let me give my father and mother a farewell

kiss; then I will follow you." Elijah said to him, "Go on
21   back: what claim have I got over you?" Leaving him,
Elisha went back, took the pair of oxen, slaughtered them,
used the implements [of plowing] to cook their flesh, and
gave [it] to the people to eat. Then he left to follow Elijah,
and he became his disciple.

It is, of course, our story: the threat, real or simply paranoid, the
flight in terror through the wilderness of despair; the wonder of
sustenance in the desert; the darkness, the stillness, the strangely
comforting loneliness of the cave in which we spend a night or a
week or however long it takes for the noise and fury of our hell to
subside; the perception of the gift, now, of gentle silence; the miracle, then, of the discovery anew of the "isness" of the Word, but
the immediate, bitter protest against it because it will not let us
stay in this place of haven from storm, this realm of the silence of
gentleness, because it sends us back again, and because it rebukes
the pride of our paranoia, our monumental sense of absolutely
unique commitment and persecution; and finally our return, to
call an Elisha on the way and to resume the work of discipleship
ministry to Word of God and word of earth, renewed by the
whole kaleidoscopic experience of the trip to the Cave.

On the Way to the Cave: vv. 2-6a, 8

*(V. 2) Now Jezebel sent this word to Elijah: "If you are Elijah, I am
Jezebel!"*

This is verse 2 of the chapter. With very considerable critical
support, verse 1 is omitted as a secondary and artificial link
between chapters 17–18 and chapter 19. The present verse 1
reports that Ahab told the whole Carmel story to Jezebel. I
don't protest the order of the chapters but suspect, along with a
lot of others who have worked this through, that this Cave narrative was originally independent of the sequences of the

drought in 17–18. And Jezebel's message is as it is preserved in the Septuagint, the Greek translation of Hebrew scripture completed in the closing centuries of the pre-Christian era. That text presupposes the magnificent and, one suspects, authentic Hebrew line: "If you are Elijah, then I am Jezebel"; you may be a prophet, but I am royalty; your name may mean "God is Yahweh," but as long as I'm here neither you nor Yahweh will stand in the kingdom of this royal house!

Make your own appropriations. Here are some of mine. It's a beautiful Saturday morning in Nanking. I'm attending Hillcrest American School and boarding with a missionary couple near retirement, their kids long since grown. It's a matter of dispute between them and me whether I'm supposed to practice the piano on Saturday. I haven't this morning. I've gone out to play. I'm ten years old. Mrs. Wilson, furious, calls me into the house. "If you are Davie, I am Mrs. Wilson." My parents are summoned from Chinkiang, two hours by rail down the Yangtze, and I am put to bed on bread and water for the rest of the weekend. (I am devastated for Saturday, but secretly I do not mind missing the long Sunday in church.) The trip to the Cave was real, but short.

Years later, 1939. I am in seminary, third year, Christmas vacation near. Failing vision in my left eye; detachment of the retina; immediate operation at Johns Hopkins and possible abandonment of projected Ph.D. program in Old Testament. "If you are Davie, I am Adversity." The trip to the Cave was longer.

It is the late 1940s. I am the teaching chaplain at the University of Georgia. It is, of course, before the Supreme Court decision of 1954 and the Martin Luther King, Jr. era of the 1960s. My wife, Joy, and I host a seminar of mine—all white, of course—for dinner and, as it turned out, a very long evening's discussion with three black Morehouse faculty, George Kelsey in Christian Ethics, A. E. Jones in French, and Ed Williams in Economics. An influential university colleague learns of it and confronts me in fury: "You *ate* with niggers? I'll have you fired if it's the last thing I do!" If you are Davie, I am Bill. (Even, then, he couldn't do it: Dr. Harmon Caldwell, then president, stood firm, and, for the time, courageously in my support.)

Now it is the 1950s. I am on the faculty of the Yale Divinity School, collaborating with a colleague at another seminary on what is to be a jointly written introduction to the Old Testament. Suddenly in the midst of the venture he writes, in effect, Your stuff is too inferior to mine to be published with it. "If you are Davie, I am (shall we say) Egbert." On that one too I went to the Cave, where the Word, and my wife, Joy, and my colleague, Richard Niebuhr, sent me back to publish that same stuff in my first book, *From Faith to Faith*.

It is 1967. I am an outspoken university chaplain and I have offended the university's conservative constituency, including the president. The very simple message: "If you are the chaplain, I am the president." The issue then centered on Vietnam, the bitter opposition to it and its effects by the vast majority of students, and the role of the chapel as the center of the resistance. Years later, when he was no longer president and I was on my way elsewhere, but U.S. personnel were still waging the war, he dropped by my office, fell glumly into a chair, and said, "Davie, what are we going to do about this damned war?"

It is 1990. We are living in Southern California. One of the chaplains at Sacred Heart Hospital in Eugene, Oregon, calls to say that our son, John (born in 1946), is in surgery and near death as a result of an auto accident. We, my wife Joy and I, fly up in time to see him brought into Intensive Care after seven hours with seven surgeons in the operating room. We are told (we do not need to be told) that he may not survive. "If you are Joy and Davie, I am Accident/Adversity." This time it was a three weeks' vigil through the desert to the Cave, and for John, years in recovery.

This is to illustrate, autobiographically, something of the variety of the form of the trauma, Elijah/Jezebel, that may send us, running for life as it were, through the desert to the Cave.

(Vv. 3-4) Frightened for his life, he [Elijah] ran away; and when he got to Beersheba in Judah, he left his servant there and went on himself for a day into the wilderness; until at last he sat down under a broom tree and prayed that he might die. "I've had it, Yahweh," he said, "Take my life: I'm no better than those who have gone before me."

Elijah: God person, Yahweh prophet, drought manager, theological persuader—this Elijah is terrified, literally scared out of his wits and running for his life. It is interesting and understandable that in the history of Elijah tradition, "fear" was changed to "awareness"—a simple alteration in vowels in Hebrew—so that the mighty prophet is represented as running away not because he is frightened but because he "sees"; he is prudently aware of Jezebel's implicit threat. Elijah's fear only serves to bring him closer to us. Our being in discipleship—as Elijah and his narrators know very well—provides us in the faith with neither doubtlessness nor fearlessness, and our total servanthood ministry, like Elijah's, is enhanced by our acknowledgment of full susceptibility to all the natural shocks that flesh and faith are heir to.

Some suggest that Elijah is suicidal.[1] I wonder. There may well be a little Semitic-Oriental hyperbole here, as also in the Moses saga, when Moses says, If this is the way it is to be, then take my life (see Numbers 11:15). Elijah is devastated, in despair, and shattered. He knows the not uncharacteristic prophetic wish, then and now, to be decommissioned. You can have the whole thing, Yahweh, he says. Carry on, Yahweh—but count me out. Go ahead with your fight, but *ohne mich*. And dear God, don't we all know this! So let's get it out, with a proper prayer, not a conventionally pious prayer like, you know, "O Lord, I'm courageous; only help my uncourage." We ought to be able to say, "Yahweh, eternal God, Lord of my Lord Jesus Christ, I've had all of Jezebel I can stand! Get her off my back! And if you can't do that, then I say the whole deal stinks, and I want out! I've had it, Yahweh. I'm no better than my mothers, my fathers, my ancestors, those who have gone before me. It is enough. . . . Take my life, since, God knows, I am not better than they."

(Vv. 5, 6a, 8) He lay down there and went to sleep; until suddenly someone touched him and said, "Wake up and eat." He looked about—and there at his head was a stone-baked biscuit and a jar of water. So he ate and drank and then, on the strength of that nourishment, he went on to Horeb.

The present text reads, by later insertion, that Elijah went "forty days and forty nights" to Horeb. This is a well-meaning, but bungling and imprecise transfer from the saga of Moses, who spent forty days and forty nights on the sacred mountain (see Exodus 24:18, 34:28 and Deuteronomy 9:9-11, 18 and 10:10). This notice nevertheless testifies to the judgment of tradition that Elijah is in rank comparable to Moses.

Here we go again. Improbable ravens improbably feed us in the wadi of a dying stream. Preposterously, we are sustained in the home of a widow, herself and her son on the verge of death by starvation. How perverse of us, dearly beloved, that we are, as we are, in terror! And now, in this desert of despair, despondent enough to be at least talking suicide, someone—thank God for someone—who was it, and who told this someone of my presence here, and of my deathlike discouragement?— someone touched me, woke me out of my dreams of desertion and death, spoke to me face to face, voice to ear, person to person, and gave me food and drink. Someone. Thank God for someone!

It is a fact of our condition as Disciples/Servants, indeed a fact of the condition of faith, that we will be sustained in ways all but incredible—no, really incredible—even in our flight in terror through the wilderness of despair.

And it is "someone"; not, as the later, present expansion of the text would have it, "someone, an angel." This appositional intrusion of orthodox piety enters the text at verse 5 some time after the simple, grace-full mystery of the original narrative had already been "clarified" with the addition of verses 6b and 7. These lines are added for the sake of the role of the angel and to accord the proper deference due this prophetic mode. According to this insertion, Elijah goes back to sleep again, to be awakened a second time not by an indefinite "someone" but by an angel of Yahweh; and this time the prophet is not only fed but verbally, sentimentally, romantically soothed: Eat now, sweet prophet, because you've got to make it all the way to the Cave! If we know what it is to live on raven food and widow fare, we can accept gracefully the grace of God from any "someone" who proffers it. The "someone" of the original text in any case makes a better angel.

Consistently now, the fare of disciples in crisis is or ought to be simple, modest, perhaps even frugal—although how many of us can lay claim to that? Here, it is water to drink; and to eat, a biscuit, a scone, a small piece of dough baked on the hot stones. The Hebrew word is *'ugah*, and we get some notion of its meagerness when Hosea denounces Ephraim as a little piece of dough cooked on only one side; literally, a half-baked *'ugah* (see Hosea 7:8).[2]

It is, of course, the profound point of this scene of the narrative that on the strength, if need be in crisis, only of a little bread and water, Elijah and we go on to Horeb.

The Stay at the Cave:
vv. 9a, 11b, 12-15a, 18

(V. 9a) Coming there [Mount Horeb] to a cave, he spent the night.

If we may presume now to clear away editorial additions from subsequent traditionists whose spontaneous but misconceived aim it was to enhance the splendor of the theophany and bring it into conformity with Mosaic saga (see Exodus 19:16, 33:22 and 34:6), then we have before us a description that is incomparably eloquent by virtue precisely of economy, simplicity, and, in all of biblical literature, stark singularity. Time stands quite still. It is a moment of crisis majestically detached from all known and common ways, and it is recounted in Hebrew without the use of a single verb to sap the naked power of static, substantive words. We can get by in English using only the imperfect of the verb "to be," but the Hebrew remains starker, barer, more powerful, more arresting:

(V. 11b) There was a mighty wind
Not in the wind was Yahweh

And after the wind earthquake
Not in the earthquake was Yahweh

(V. 12) And after the earthquake fire
Not in the fire was Yahweh

And after the fire—
A sound of gentle silence.

This reading omits, again with nearly unanimous critical support, verses 9b-10, an almost identical duplication of verses 13b-14. The question "What are you doing here, Elijah?" and his response are appropriate only after he emerges from the cave. The command of verse 11a to "stand before Yahweh" is also premature; and what immediately follows, the notice that "Yahweh passed by," is an import from Mosaic theophanies where Yahweh manifests himself in these very physical phenomena:

> Now at daybreak two days later, there were peals of thunder and flashes of lightning, dense cloud on the mountain and a very loud trumpet blast. . . . Mount Sinai [Horeb] was entirely wrapped in smoke, because Yahweh had descended on it in the form of fire. The smoke rose like smoke from a furnace and the whole mountain shook violently. . . . Moses spoke, and God answered him in the thunder.

> [Again Moses said], "Please show me your glory." Yahweh said, "I shall make all my goodness pass before you. . . . But my face . . . you cannot see, for no human being can see me and survive. . . . [But] here is a place near me. You will stand on the rock, and when my glory passes by, I shall put you in a cleft of the rock and shield you with my hand until I have gone past. Then I shall take my hand away and you will see my back; but my face will not be seen." (Exodus 19:16, 18-19; 33:18-23 NJB)

The command to Elijah to stand before Yahweh while Yahweh passes by, as well as the phrases which enhance the violence of the wind in verse 11, are accretions all but irresistibly motivated by the fact of the coincidences of the Sinai-Horeb theophanies and by tradition's firm establishment of a kind of Moses-Elijah parity.

But all this serves only to create a contradiction in the narrative of Elijah, where we have to do not with a cleft in the rock but with the Cave, and where it is the emphatic point of the Elijah narrative, the precise point, that in the violent physical phenomena of wind, earthquake, and fire, Yahweh is not only not passing by, but that in no sense whatsoever is he even present in these phenomena. One suspects that the narrative stands as a splendid rebuke to all of those (or any of us) nature worshipers who are episodically disposed to make a theophany out of natural phenomena from sex to sunset, mountain to sea, rose to artichoke.[3]

Alas, dear hearts, it is not even the "still, small voice." When the deafening sound of the awe-full violence of nature is past and there is that sudden, contrasting gentleness of quiet, that audible voice of silence, it is the Word of Yahweh (preserved in verse 9*a*) that is, that comes, that occurs, that happens, that is articulate and apprehensible. Since a theophany is "a physical presentation or manifestation of deity . . . a brief *appearance* of deity,"[4] it is a question whether Elijah's experience on the sacred mountain is a theophany at all. Yahweh was not in wind, earthquake, or fire; and after all of these, there was a sound of gentle silence.

(V. 13) Upon hearing this, Elijah covered his face with his robe and went out to take his position at the mouth of the cave. It was only now that the Word of Yahweh was [that is, that it came, that it occurred, that it happened, that it was articulate and apprehensible]: *"What are you doing here, Elijah?"*

"Mah-lecha poh 'eliyahu?"

Elijah replied. . . .

Now watch the defense mechanism come into play. Elijah is of course taken aback. He is affronted. What kind of Yahweh Word is this, this implicit rebuff? Doesn't he understand that it's this damned prophetic role of his that brings me here to the Cave, shattered, exhausted, running and hiding for my very life? I don't need this critical-interrogating Word; I need the healing Word, the affirming Word, the stroking Word.

(V. 14) *Elijah replied* [to that seemingly uninformed, unsympathetic Word, Elijah replied testily]: *"I have been passionately devoted to Yahweh, God of hosts, even while the people of Israel have abandoned you. Your altars they have destroyed, your prophets they have put to death with the sword. I am left now, myself, alone; and they are after me to take my life!"*

One can hear it on occasion from any parish minister in the land or from any of us disciple/servants "beset behind and before." Yahweh's Lone Ranger . . . Horatio at the Bridge . . . Hans Brinker with his silver skates and his finger in the dike (or was that somebody else?) . . . the last single remaining bastion of theological and prophetic integrity . . . and, for background music, the *Tannhaüser* Overture. Don't you understand: they are after me!

(V. 15a) *But Yahweh answered* [Elijah]: *"Go back the way you have come. . . ."*

I'm omitting verses 15*b*, 16, and 17, the tri-commission to anoint two kings and a prophet: Hazael over Syria, Jehu over Israel, and Elisha to succeed Elijah himself. The late Professor James Montgomery, whose commentary on Kings published posthumously under the editorship of Henry Gehman was the last volume in the distinguished series, *The International Critical Commentary*, writes of these verses and the commission:

> This sequel remains a standing puzzle. Elijah did not anoint Hazael and Jehu; it was Elisha [who] suggested to Hazael the murder of his predecessor (II Kings 8:7ff.), and who indirectly anointed Jehu (9:1ff.). The alleged commission to Elijah appears to be a case of transfer from the Elisha legend.[5]

To which I would simply add that even the commission to "anoint" Elisha is spurious: aside from the single instance of Isaiah 61:1, where the reference is probably only metaphorical,[6] there is no evidence whatsoever that the practice of anointing prophets existed in ancient Israel.

(Vv. 15a, 18) *Yahweh answered* [Elijah]: *"Go back the way you have*

come. . . . Retrace your steps; return to where and what you were because there are still seven thousand left in Israel [the number is no census count but a round number, "thousands upon thousands"] *whose knees have never bent to Baal, nor whose lips have kissed him!"*

The way to the cave or, to broaden the metaphor, the ways to the caves are as crowded these U.S. years as roads to the beaches on Labor Day weekend. Why have we become a generation of cave seekers? Well, if Elijah is legion, then so is Jezebel; and if Jezebel is legion, so is the cave.

As the flight to the cave is undertaken by vast numbers for a vast range of reasons, so too the nature of the cave varies vastly and appropriately. Nevertheless, every search for the cave represents the more or less desperate craving of the searcher for relief from coping with the seemingly uncopeable. The cave is the womb.

A few of the obvious drives that pack us off, daily or weekly or episodically or, for some, in hope, permanently, are fear or even terror in the particular given set of circumstances; the sheer discouragement and exhaustion of facing questions without answer; profound disillusionment—it takes many forms—with the pertinent, prevailing system or systems; deep and bitter contempt for one's own society, bred of its abysmal failure to attain in consistent practice even a semblance of the justice professed and acclaimed; despair over the formidable obduracy of a political establishment in going its merciless way quite apparently deaf to the cries of anguish of its empathetic and real victims, victims by the tens of millions here and around the world.

"What are you doing here, Elijah?"

The traffic to the cave may embrace us all, rich and poor, royalty and commoner, black, brown and white, free and slave, female and male, peasant and landowner, exploiter and oppressed—and all of us bent on exchanging what we deem to be an unremediable, intolerable, essentially uninhabitable situation for peace—or even the illusion of peace. And the range of caves runs from the old standbys of sex and alcohol and other drugs to TA (Transactional Analysis), TM (Transcendental

Meditation), TV (before whom, on an average, we stand, sit, lie, eat, and drink an unconscionable and unbelievable number of adult hours per week), TF (touchy-feely in dual or group encounters), TZ (try Zen), TS (take sedatives), or even, in some circles, TJ (take Jesus—in this sense an icon distantly derived from Jesus Christ), and literally scores of others.

And one more cave in the "T" series, TB—turn back; turn back to the past; if we can't hold it intact in every present we can return to it. I'm told—I don't know this—that the most popular song surviving from the Beatles era is "Yesterday." ("I believe in yesterday.") It is possible to go even farther back into the cave. A San Francisco columnist, writing of the accession of a recent president said of him, "He likes things to be the way they were the day before yesterday."

Now, it is not my intention to say that the cave has no legitimate function. Elijah came back from the cave revived, renewed. Although the Word of Yahweh appears to have been absent and silent in the cave, the experience of the cave, the recapitulation of the womb, the distance and perspective afforded by the cave from and upon Baalism and Jezebel and People—all this was and is a legitimate gift of the legitimate and essential cave trip. It may be given to us, to all Elijahs, to return from the cave with fear and terror, if not allayed, at least in control; with new resources given to face unanswerable questions with courage and endurance; with disillusionment transformed to fresh determination; with societal contempt converted again to sorrow, compassion, and resolution; and with despair turning back once more to prophetic passion.

I hope it is unnecessary to say that both the church and the seminary suffer erosion of authenticity in proportion to the measure of their acquiescence in institutional cave-playing. Many, lay and clergy, would make the church the cave, the escape, the refuge, the womb. The resources of faith, which by the grace of God are imparted to the church as gifts to be given and proclaimed, are themselves such, properly dispensed, as to render infrequent or unnecessary the trip to the cave. But the church itself may not be the cave, except at the cost of losing both the Word of God and the word of earth.

So, too, the seminary, where we must look harder and more

critically than we have in the past at applicants who are clearly seeking not a theological education but in fact the cave. It was a practicing New York psychoanalyst and an adjunct seminary instructor, who said not many years ago that we in the seminaries have been admitting too many theological students with high dependency needs and with consequently sustained and often serious psychological problems. He calls for the admission not of unturbulent people but of men and women, in his words, "who see the ministry more as a mission than [as] a haven."[7] It remains a fact of contemporary seminary existence in North America that too many of our students (and faculty) demand of the theological institution that it be the cave, and remain bitterly and vocally critical of it when and as it declines so to function.

For all the legitimacy of the cave trip, the Word that comes when we emerge from the cave where alone the Word is accessible to us—the Word that comes is always the same: "What are you doing here? Do you know what you are doing here? And, if you know why you have come, then go back to what and where and who you were."

Paulo Freire says that we "are not built in silence, but in word, in work, in action-reflection." And in a note on that statement he comments:

> I obviously do not refer to the silence of profound meditation [could we say, the cave], in which [one] only apparently leaves the world, withdrawing from it in order to consider it in its totality, and thus remaining with it. But this type of retreat is only authentic when the meditator is "bathed" in reality; not when the retreat signifies . . . flight from [the world], in a type of "historical schizophrenia."[8]

"What are you doing here, Elijah?" You may stay overnight, as it were, in the cave; but you may not *stay* in the cave, shut off from the word of earth, and so from Word of God. This is the very Word of God: Go back now, to hear and heed the word of earth!

Do we understand in the church as disciples/servants what Freire is talking about when he says that people "cannot save themselves (no matter how one understands 'salvation'), either as individuals or as an oppressor class? Salvation can be achieved only with others."[9]

And it is Rosemary Ruether who suggests that there are two ways falsely to appropriate the transcendent. One is to domesticate it; the other is to separate it, isolate the Word, cut it away from the whole of human life. "Both the establishment [domestication] of Christianity and the segregation of the sacred to a sphere removed from the midst of life are equally ways of abolishing the presence of the Holy Spirit, so that the world of the powers and principalities can go on as before."[10]

Domestication is the double altar. It is Baalism. The attempt at sustained separation is cavism, tolerable, acceptable, even therapeutic as temporary expedient, but quickly self-defeating since word of earth and, in consequence, Word of God are shut away.

"What are you doing here, Elijah? . . . Go back the way you have come; because there are still seven thousand [thousands upon thousands, a multitude, vast throngs] . . . whose knees have never bent to Baal, nor whose lips have kissed him!"

The Way Back from the Cave (vv. 19-21)

It is possible, as an occasional textual critic has suggested, and as The New Jerusalem Bible footnotes, that the closing verses of I Kings 19 are transferred or borrowed from the Elisha cycle of stories. Be that as it may, these lines offer a sharply appropriate climax to the narrative of the Cave.

(Vv. 19-21) Leaving that place. . . .
Leaving the cave. . . .
[Elijah] came upon Elisha son of Shaphat plowing with twelve yoke of oxen in front of him, and he was with the twelfth. As Elijah passed by, he tossed his robe over him. Leaving the oxen . . .
The Hebrew term may be stronger than this. "Leaving" sug-

gests that Elisha may momentarily return. But the verb probably connotes the act of forswearing, of abandonment of all that is represented in *habaqar*, the oxen or, better, the cattle, as the symbol of the life and work from which now Elisha means to separate himself, permanently and with finality. His very brief return, in a moment, is a ritual performance of that intention.

Leaving the oxen, [Elisha] ran after Elijah and said, "Let me give my father and mother a farewell kiss; then I will follow you." Elijah said to him, "Go on back; what claim have I got over you?" Leaving him, Elisha went back, took the pair of oxen, slaughtered them, used the implements [of plowing] to cook their flesh, and gave [it] to the people to eat. Then he left to follow Elijah, and he became his disciple.

Don't misunderstand me, which may be a way of saying to myself—don't let me misunderstand me. The cave may be good, recreative, restorative, and therefore essential; but not cavism, which would institutionalize the cave. Cave, *sí*; cavism, *no*! The cave gives shelter when the furies without and within are raging beyond all control, and the Word comes more easily and distinctly after the grateful sound of gentle silence and our emergence from this place of isolation and security. It is now that we know, in the Word of God and the word of earth, that we are not alone, that we are surrounded in fact by clouds of living witnesses, that there is the work of the kingdom to be done, and disciples and colleagues, intimate Elishas, with whom to be doing the work.

Go back. Always go back; and on the way, always on the way, find, commission, enlist, and inspire Elisha and Elisha and Elisha. Go—with the Word of God and the word of earth.

Go, with Elijah and Elisha. Go, with Gustavo Gutiérrez, who would bid us be mindful of that great company of anonymous Christians who, unable for compelling reasons to name the name of Yahweh/Christ, are nevertheless among the thousands who have not and will not bow down to Baal; and who reminds us that, in Christ, God is "irreversibly committed to the present moment [he means, of course, every present moment] to carry it to its fulfillment."[11]

Go with Elijah and Elisha.

Go with Dom Helder Camara, who, on rare and intimate

terms with the bitter word of Brazilian earth as well as with the Word of God, was nevertheless able to declare:

> I believe in a Creator . . . who desired man [and woman] as co-Creators and who gave [them] intelligence and a creative imagination to complete the Creation . . . and [God] constantly sends [the Holy] Spirit to make the human mind fruitful, even as [God] made the waters fertile at the beginning of Creation.[12]

Go with Elijah and Elisha—and with Paulo Freire, who, against odds much greater than we see or know, affirms his trust, as he says simply, "in the people," and his faith "in the creation of a world in which it will be easier to love."[13]

Go with Rainer Maria Rilke, too, who on August 12, 1904, wrote from Sweden to a young poet he never met (what a good Elijah person he was!):

> We must assume our existence as broadly as we in any way can; everything, even the unheard of, must be possible in it. That is at bottom the only courage that is demanded of us; to have courage for the most strange, the most singular and the most inexplicable that we may encounter. That [humankind] has in this sense been cowardly has done life endless harm; the experiences that are called "vision," the whole so-called "spirit-world," death, all those things that are so closely akin to us, have by daily parrying been so crowded out of life that the senses with which we could have grasped them are atrophied. To say nothing of God.[14]

In the same letter he writes, "We have no reason to mistrust our world, for it is not against us [Rilke too has heard the rebuke at the mouth of the Cave]. If it has terrors, they are our terrors; if it has abysses, those abysses belong to us; [and] if there are dangers at hand, we must try to love them."[15]

Go with Elijah and Elisha. Go with all these. Go even with Gary MacEoin's conscientized Latin-American priests who choose to stay within the church and who do not, he writes, "see themselves as conduits of grace to tens of thousands of people. They are satisfied if they can create a few small islands of Christian life, leaving the future radiation to the Holy Spirit."[16]

We will go to the cave as we may and must when the time

and place of our present moment become unendurable, when, in whatever way, we hear the terrifying word of threatened, unqualified disaster: If you are Elijah, I am Jezebel! But we will take only temporary lodging there. We will resist the drift or the drive toward cavism in ourselves, in the church, and in the life of faith. On our way, always on our way in the earth, we will bring Elisha with us to the work of the Word of God and the word of earth; if we cannot do more—it is enough—we will help create islands of authentic Christian life, and we will be content in faith to leave the future radiation to the Holy Spirit.

CHAPTER FOUR

The Inheritance

(I Kings 21, author translation)

1   Now it happened that one Naboth of Jezreel owned a vine-
2   yard adjacent to Ahab's [winter] residence; until one day
    Ahab made this offer to Naboth: "Let me have your vine-
    yard to use as a vegetable garden, since it immediately
    adjoins my property. In exchange, I will give you a better
3   vineyard, or, if you prefer, I will pay you its worth in
    cash." But Naboth replied to Ahab, "Yahweh forbid that I
    should give you my ancestral inheritance!"

4   So Ahab returned home sullen and seething over Naboth's
    refusal to relinquish his ancestral inheritance. He lay
    down on his bed, averted his face, and refused to eat any-
    thing.

5   But then his wife, Jezebel, came to him and said, "What
6   has you so upset that you won't [even] eat anything?" So
    he told her, "I made a proposal to Naboth. I said to him,
    'Give me your vineyard for cash or, if you prefer, I will
    give you a vineyard in exchange for it.' But he said, 'I will
    not give you my vineyard.'"

7   His wife, Jezebel, answered him, "Do you or do you not
    exercise rule over Israel? Snap out of it, eat something, and
    take heart! I will myself present you with Naboth's vine-
    yard!"

8   Accordingly, she wrote letters in Ahab's name, sealing
    them with his seal; and she sent the letters to the elders
9   and freemen who were Naboth's fellow council members.
11 This was the message: "Proclaim a fast, with Naboth
12 presiding over the convocation." They did as Jezebel told

13 them to do; they proclaimed a fast and set Naboth over the assembly. But now two men sitting near him testified against Naboth before the people with the charge, "Naboth cursed God and king!" So they took him out of town and stoned him to death.

14 The message was sent to Jezebel that Naboth had been

15 stoned and was dead; and as soon as Jezebel received it, she said to Ahab, "Go ahead now; take possession of Naboth's vineyard which he refused to give you for [hard]

16 cash. For Naboth no longer lives: he is dead!" Immediately at the word of Naboth's death, Ahab started on his way to take possession of Naboth's vineyard.

17 But the Word of Yahweh occurred, and spoke to Elijah:

18 "Be on your way now to confront Ahab king of Israel; you will find him in Naboth's vineyard where he has gone to take possession of it. You will give him this message:

19 'Thus says Yahweh: Having murdered, do you even now take possession? In the place where the dogs licked Naboth's blood they shall lick your blood!'"

20 Ahab said to Elijah, "Have you found me, O my enemy?" Elijah replied, "I have found you."

A Rilke Word

Some years ago a seminary student in one of my classes wrote in a paper on the Call of Isaiah (Isaiah 6):

> Would that the terms of my own call were so plain and pronounced. It would seem that one could hardly be half-hearted or uncertain about one's mission if one were given marching orders against a backdrop of tremors and smoke and seraphic adoration. I'd say that Isaiah got a good deal.

All of us who know, in varied ways, the call to discipleship are well aware of what this seminarian is talking about. In his *Letters to a Young Poet*, Rainer Maria Rilke at least twice insists on his own inadequacy or vulnerability, and in some appropriate way I would like to claim the sense of his demurrers. In the beginning of the second letter, explaining that he is still recovering from an illness, he says that "writing comes hard to me, and so you must take these few lines for more."[1] My own lines in these essays have not come easy, and I pray that by your own appropriation of them, and by the power of the Holy Spirit brooding always among us, you may receive them as more than given.

Rilke's eighth letter concludes, "Do not believe that he who seeks to comfort you lives untroubled. . . . His life has much difficulty and sadness and remains far behind yours. Were it otherwise he would never have been able to find these words."[2] This is not to say that it has been my intention only to comfort you, but rather that if and when I may have spoken in such a way as to appear to be without doubt and frustration and anguish, it has to do with the stance that the occasion of writing thrusts upon me.

Word of God, Word of Earth

These are not times in which comfort is easily come by; or, if it is, it may be insubstantial, or bought in a corrupt transaction of exchange of Word of God and word of earth for the obsessive word of the trivial, encapsulated world in which one is oneself the undisputed center. Take, for example, the case of the successful young man writing in *Guideposts* magazine from his home in Palm Beach, Florida, in a feature called "A Spiritual Workshop" and titled, "How to Begin a Glorious Day." I quote this in disapproval not so much of what is said, but of what is not said. This piece is one-dimensional, parochial. It belongs with other expressions of essential privatism.

> I open my eyes. It is 5 A.M. I slide from the bed to my knees and pray before quickly slipping on some shorts, a sweat shirt, socks

165

and jogging shoes. It's still dark outside when I open the front door. A warm breeze is blowing in from the ocean.

Soon I am jogging along Route A-1-A, beside the ocean. . . . As I jog along, I begin my spiritual exercise.

"Thank You, Lord, for this day. . . . " I thank Him for strong legs and a healthy body. In prayer, I review all my blessings.

My prayer turns to people. Loved ones, friends, business contacts. I name them out loud, those near and far. And then our leaders, "Lord, give them courage to take a stand for You."

The miles tick off. Two golden shafts come strong out of the sea and fade away into the morning sky. They remind me of a giant ladder which leads up to the heavens. Jacob dreamed of a ladder which went to Heaven and there at the top was the Lord, who told Jacob, "I am with thee." I meditate on that.

"Be with me, Lord," I pray. . . .

An orange ball appears at the rim of the ocean. The two golden poles of the ladder split into multi-colored shafts of light. The vast panorama across the eastern sky is changing.

I am back home now, refreshed and strengthened for a glorious new day.[3]

This is an experience of earth, to be sure—ocean, beach, the spectacular light of the sun as refracted through the earth's atmosphere, and the feet of the young jogger beating strongly, steadily, against the face of the ground. But it is an experience that has little, if anything, to do with the word of earth; it is an exercise that may in fact be calculated to shut out, to shut away, the real word of earth. And if it is an experience of God, it is god with a small "g," an idolatrous experience, self-aggrandizing, titillating, not far removed from the sensuousness of Baalism, over against which Elijah stands.

In any case, how far removed is this self-contented jogger from the authentic apprehension of Word of God and word of earth. Dom Helder Camara, the diminutive Brazilian archbishop, who in an earlier decade symbolized Christian opposition to military dictatorship not only in Brazil but throughout Latin America, was awarded an honorary doctorate of laws at Harvard University in 1974. The citation might have read, "For rare and courageous sensitivity and commitment to Word of God and word of earth." It read, in fact, "The most Reverend Helder Camara, Doctor of Laws. A tireless opponent of poverty and injustice, a stalwart Christian leader offering life and hope to the downtrodden and defeated."[4]

It was an event ignored, of course, in Brazil. And even Harvard gave him no chance to deliver the speech he had prepared for the occasion. But *Harvard Magazine* reported it, and *Christianity and Crisis* printed it.[5] His words point out the utter vacuity of the jogger's "religious" intoxication, and they are as powerful and pertinent now as they were when first written.

He said the pessimist in him mocked his receipt of a degree in law when "law is ever more a hollow word, resonant but empty, in a world increasingly dominated by force, by violence, by fraud, by injustice, by avarice—in a word, by egoism"; when civil law permits "the progressive and rapid increase of oppressed people who continue being swept toward ghettos, without work, without health, without instruction, without diversion and, not rarely, without God"; when under so-called international law "more than two-thirds of humanity [exist] in situations of misery, of hunger, of subhuman life"; and when agrarian law or spatial law permits "today's powerful landowners to continue to live at the cost of misery for unhappy pariahs"; and whereby "modern technology achieves marvels from the earth with an ever-reduced number of rural workers [while] those not needed in the fields live sublives in depressing slums on the outskirts of nearly all the large cities."

Dom Helder spoke of "subwork leading to sublife . . . of the greed of multinationals that export entire factories to paradises of investment where salaries are low and dispute impossible. . . ."

Dom Helder Camara: word of earth.

The speech ends on the note of the Word of God in response to the word of earth:

> The degree with which you honor me brings me to ask of God that at this point of life . . . I spend myself to the end in the service of humankind—as the most secure means of giving glory to our Lord.

> God permit that the symbol of my life be a candle that burns itself, that consumes itself while there is still wax to burn; when nothing more remains to be consumed, that my flame, yet an

instant, dare to remain alive and afoot, to rumble after, happy in the conviction that one day the force of Right will conquer the pretended right of force.[6]

Word of God, word of earth!

On Adjacency

This Jezreel event[7] of coveted adjacent property and of subsequent treachery and murder for the sake of possession—this particular crisis of adjacency happened in the middle of the ninth century before our era. With variation, but in essential correspondence of members of the plot, it happened of course throughout the spreading human family in the centuries and years, perhaps even months or days, preceding; and it has most assuredly continued to happen, in its significant essence, with persistence and always accompanying human carnage down to our own time and decade and, who knows, even day and hour. It may be happening even among us today or yesterday or tomorrow, on a simpler scale, of course, with covetousness, treachery, murder, and possession all symbolized in aggression against the psyche of another, an adjacent *person*. The resultant human carnage in such a case takes the form of a sophisticated psychological increment to a sustained, subtle process of essential dehumanization of a spouse or colleague or anyone in the array of personal relationships.

The recurrent phenomenon may be described as the problem of adjacency. Let us call the two parties A and B. B's property or treasure, B's heritage, B's right, is adjacent, or appears to be adjacent, or is declared to be adjacent to A's. Adjacency is a phenomenally flexible term, subject to interpretation according to what is deemed to be adjacent by the powerful covetor; B's thing which is B's by rights, by inheritance, becomes in its adjacency an object of passionate desire, an obsessive craving, on the part of a more powerful A. In the classical expression of the problem of adjacency, of which the story before us is a splendid example, the ensuing conflict of interest between A and B proves to be irreconcilable, and the weaker B is effectively eliminated as a contender. This is done, in this remarkable human family of which we are all a part, with demonic craft by the powerful, in an absolutely dazzling array of forms (if necessity is the mother of invention, covetousness and lust are the parents of ingenuity), upon well-established but shamelessly fraudulent justification, usually in the broad sense religious and sometimes even specifically theological. The more heinous the perpetuation of violence issuing from the problem of adjacency, the more probable, not to say imperative, the establishment of grounds in essential piety. This is to ensure the crucial support ostensibly of God himself (one suspects A always knows better), but, failing that, at least the consent of the rank and file of God's would-be worshipers.

In practice, of course, problems of adjacency are often resolved by the capitulation of B. I cannot speak for you, but if I had been in Naboth's place I think I would certainly have been tempted to say, What is this inheritance of mine or what do I care about my right when looked at over against what my refusal may cost me, or what I may gain by currying favor with the powerful A, and by striking with him an advantageous deal into the bargain? But this is not Naboth.

Olive Schreiner, an Englishwoman of South Africa, born in the middle of the nineteenth century and surviving well into the twentieth, was in many perceptive ways vastly ahead of her time. Of the sensitive English persons of her own place and generation she wrote, "We know, none so well, how stained is our African record; we know with what envious eyes the Government of English Ahabs eyes the patrimony of Black Naboths and takes it, if necessary, after bearing false witness against Naboth."[8] The government of U.S. Ahabs has followed and outstripped the English lead. Like the claim of the old British Empire, we too can say that the sun never sets on fields and lands, on kingdoms and governments, on men and women and children, on myriads of Naboths—all "adjacent" to us.

We play the grim game of adjacency with our own oppressed minorities and, as well, whether with Naboth's capitulation or elimination, with populations—what a monstrous litany!—

169

from Mexico to Guatemala to Chile; from Korea and Vietnam to Grenada, Nicaragua, Honduras and El Salvador; from Puerto Rico to Cuba to Panama; and all the way to Saudi Arabia, Kuwait, Iraq, and the Persian Gulf. In fact, of course, Naboth's vineyard, "adjacent" to U.S. property, is a global phenomenon; and at least since the administration of James Monroe (1817-1825) we have in devious ways so misrepresented circumstances to fit our charges, or so created false charges outright, as to justify invasion, co-optation, murder and even possession. The terms of accusation are capable of quite remarkable variation: "Naboth cursed God and the king!"

And when, on relatively rare occasion, the mighty U.S. Ahab has been thwarted in having his way, the frustrated administration has withdrawn, sullen and seething, with face steadfastly averted—until a new, diverting, "successful" venture in "National Security" presents itself.

We know, none so well, how stained is our national record; we know with what envious eyes our transnational and military and political Ahabs even yet regard the inheritance of Third World Naboths, and how we continue to move to secure the fruits of that inheritance—more often than not by swearing false witness against Naboth.

By Violation and Violence

Elijah's successor prophets in the next century decry the lust for adjacent land; and they do so, of course, among a people in whose corporate understanding inherited property is a part of one's "psychological totality."[9] Several decades ago, Johannes Pedersen called attention to

> the terror ringing through [Naboth's] answer to the proposal of the king. . . . Naboth cannot part with the property which he has inherited from his [ancestors] without committing sacrilege against himself and his kindred, so closely do kindred and property belong together. . . . In all the laws of the Old Testament it is taken absolutely for granted that no one sells . . . landed property without being forced to do so.[10]

It is this sense of the identity of person and property that intensifies Isaiah's denunciation of those "who join house to house, who add field to field" (Isaiah 5:8). And whether the juxtaposition is editorial or not, this cry of woe follows immediately upon the concluding verse of the "Song of the Vineyard":

> The vineyard of the LORD of hosts
>   is the house of Israel,
> and the people of Judah
>   are his pleasant planting;
> he expected justice,
>   but saw bloodshed;
> righteousness,
>   but heard a cry!
>
> (Isaiah 5:7)

Micah's indictment is characteristically even more passionate (and one almost wonders whether both prophets explode as they do impelled, even if unconsciously, by the then already classical model (of the Naboth incident). The Revised English Bible puts it this way:

> Woe betide those who lie in bed
>   planning evil and wicked deeds,
> and rise at daybreak to do them,
>   knowing that they have the power to do evil!
> They covet fields and take them by force;
> if they want a house they seize it;
> they lay hands on both householder and house,
> on a man and all he possesses.
>
> (Micah 2:1-2 REB)

It was Jezebel who planned and executed the evil by which not only Naboth's inheritance, but also his very life was taken. To the brooding king—this product of the religion of Baal, devoid of Yahwism's sense of justice and righteousness—she says, "Do you or do you not exercise rule over Israel!" There is an insinuation of incredulity laced with disdain and scorn. The German Roman Catholic scholar A Šanda admirably paraphrases, "Du bist mir ein feiner König!" "A fine king you are for me!"[11] Knowing that we Ahabs and Jezebels have the power, and wanting Naboth's land and inheritance, we will

171

take it by force of violence; but we will see to it that our punishment of Naboth fits his "crime" against us. As he in the name of
Yahweh refused us the acquisition of vineyard, so we, in the
name of that same Yahweh, will do away with Naboth and
seize his inheritance.[12]

In the Name of God

It is, alas, all too devastating a parable of our own times and
kingdoms; of our own pentagons, war departments, international peddlers of arms; of our own multinational corporations;
of our own and allied governments. In the primary, if not sole,
interest of maintaining and enhancing what we possess—in
this world in truth like a royal residence and grounds in
Jezreel—we plan our evil deeds and rise at daybreak to do
them, knowing that we have the power; and what we covet we
will acquire be it even another's inheritance of life, of dignity,
of humanity. We will appropriate what is Naboth's to have and
to hold from this day forward, for better, for worse, to love and
to cherish, till death us do part—and we will do it ostensibly
according to God's holy ordinance.

We take it where we will and can, from our own minority
Naboths to the Naboths in the Caribbean, in Central and South
America, and on the continents of Africa and Asia. We do
what we do in the way of appropriation and, if need be, murder with all the craft of a Jezebel. We do it, by cunning, by
power and prestige, by elaborately contrived false witness—
we also do it claiming all the while that it is done in the name
of Yahweh, according to God's holy ordinance, even in the
name of Jesus Christ (and of course because we are a Christian
nation under God). You know: "In God We Trust." And so,
wherever we do it, we insist that we do it for you, you who
survive our doing it. We do it to make your world safe for
democracy (our brand of democracy, of course). We steal or
destroy your inheritance to protect you from "Godlessness"!

We do it to help you build airports and highways for your use, of course (but also so that we may the more easily exercise our prerogatives of adjacency).

And dearly beloved, I do not know how or whether we shall stop it until it is too late, even for us.

The "we" that I've been using—the first-person pronoun plural—deserves a word. Of course it is not you and I who are the instrumental perpetrators of covetous adjacency with its attendant treachery, murder, and seizure. It is not we who in any direct sense perform the act of the theft of the inheritance. I suspect that we are by and large among those whom our contemporaries on the extreme right call bleeding hearts, and they do emphatically mean that term pejoratively. They would also say of us, the bleeding hearts, that we—to exchange one metaphor for another—shed only crocodile tears. We would respond, most of us, that we do in fact bleed, that we know both outrage and anguish for what our arrogant power has inflicted and continues to inflict on lands and people near and far!

Despite the tendency of the Elijah narratives to disparage Ahab, the facts about him clearly return the impression of a man and monarch of exceptional stature. First Kings 20 and 22 see him in rather better light than chapters 17–19, and 21. Except as viewed exclusively from the perspective of Yahwist fundamentalists or fanatics, he was a person of outstanding ability, integrity, and courage. He of course desperately wanted Naboth's inheritance. He was persuaded that he needed it. He no doubt convinced himself that he deserved it, that it was somehow his right, even as advertisers, from fast-food restaurants to airline companies, seek to convince us that we deserve a break, namely, their product or service. And however acquired, Ahab hoped that once possessed the whole matter of the vineyard could be forgotten.

Jezebel goes to work and Ahab stands by, as too often too many of us do. But in this democracy of ours, pseudo or real, the arrangements for the act of possession and the essential steps of pious subterfuge, false witness, indictment without defense, and finally violence and murder—all this is, in a manner of speaking, done in our name and sealed with our seal. It is done by leaders whom we elect, with the expenditure of our tax dollars, and often with careful particularity, in alleged and ostensible concern for values purporting to be cherished among us in the religious establishment.

It is my simple and direct submission that in common practice in organized religion in the United States we have let our Jezebels set the stage for the effective dispossession of the inheritance of land, resources, productivity, and human dignity of weaker neighbors declared to be adjacent to us all around the globe. The vast majority of us in the church are able to live like relative Ahabs because Jezebel is scheming schemes and working works around the clock—in our name and, as it works out, also to our profit. And we do not want to look too closely; we cannot bring ourselves to renounce the ways of Jezebel even when we know that Naboth's vineyard is ours by treachery, violence, and murder. But woe are we, dearly beloved, we are undone, we are lost, if the church is silent, if no powerful, corporate, prophetic protest is made when in this Jezreel palace of ours there is violence instead of justice, a vast cry (increasingly bitter and militant) from the world's dispossessed, instead of justice and the practice of the right of force instead of the force of right.

The Question and the Questions

Was it really Jezebel who did it? Ahab knew, Ahab knew. Ahab always knows. Jezebel wrote letters in Ahab's name, sealing them with his seal. We know, we know. And Ahab always receives the word that Naboth's inheritance is his for the taking with grotesquely mingled feelings of satisfaction and dread. Jezebel said to Ahab, "Go ahead now; take possession of Naboth's vineyard which he refused to give you for cash. For Naboth no longer lives: he is dead!" Naboth is dispossessed. His inheritance is yours.

What is the word of earth? This is the word of earth—that Naboth is legion; that Naboth's essential inheritance, land, work, creativity, human dignity, is daily seized by the strong—and that we are now the strongest of the strong!

But the Word of God occurred, and spoke to Elijah: "Be on your way now to confront Ahab king of Israel; you will find him in Naboth's vineyard where he has gone to take possession of it. You will give him this message: 'Thus says Yahweh: Having murdered, do you even now take possession? In the place where the dogs licked Naboth's blood they shall lick your blood!'"

Question: To whom are we, church people of the United States, disciples, to whom are we preponderantly more analogous, Elijah or Ahab?

Question: Which is the more influential altar among us, that of Yahweh or of Baal, God or mammon, Christ or possessions?

Question: Is it not true that as a people we have in our whole history repeatedly and down to his present day murdered, in body but also spirit and psyche, in order to possess?

Question: Is it not true that by and large we of the church have been in consent, if not always with our ballots, then by our silence?

Question: Whose inheritance now sustains the life of relative wealth and plenty that is ours, our own (which we've spent and overspent) or that of a plurality of Naboths?

Question: Can we yet turn back the judgment that we too will die in our own blood where and because we have shed the innocent blood and seized the cherished human heritage of myriad, uncountable, unsung, powerless, and dispossessed Naboths—red, black, brown, yellow, and white?

Question: Can we revive and recreate Elijah among us; can the church, can we of the church, servants and disciples, be prophet as well as priest to king and nation and world?

Ahab said to Elijah, "Have you found me, O my enemy?"

Elijah replied, "I have found you."

Georg Fohrer best returns the sense of it:

"Hast du mich gefunden? Hast du mich endlich bei einem Verbrechen ertappt?"

Und Elia antwortet: "Ich habe dich ertappt!"

And as Fohrer adds, "Mit diesem Höhepunkt schloss die alte Erzählung."[13]

It is the sense of the German that the original narrative closed with this dramatic exchange. Ahab knew, he knew. He knew all along it wouldn't wash with Yahweh. We Ahabs always know; but there will be no confession, no turning, no cessation of the ways of Jezebel, no restitution, no redemption of the vast, total human inheritance except by the happening of the Word, its speaking again to Elijah, us, and Elijah's ministry, ours, to Ahab and Jezebel and the hordes of the always oncoming Naboths.

Have you (Fohrer's sense) at last caught me in the very act, O my enemy, my old enemy, my old friend, my old dreaded and cherished prophet; after all this, have you really uncovered me; after drought, after that contest of altars on Mount Carmel, after your flight from us in terror that took you all the way to your cave on Horeb—after all this have you caught me, exposed me, apprehended me by the Word of Yahweh, judged me in that same Word—and so, perhaps, in spite of judgment, opened the only possible way to my redemption? Have you found me, O my enemy—O Word of God, O Word of God incarnate?

And so the literal reading is best after all: I have found you. I think Ahab knew. Question: Do we? For it is only in being fully found by the Word of God that we may be saved, that we may hear and understand and heed the anguished, bitter, raucous, critical word of earth, and that the inheritance of us all may be preserved and enhanced to the glory of God and to the service of God's children of the earth.

NOTES

PART III: WORD OF GOD, WORD OF EARTH
Chapter One: The Drought
1. Rubém Alves, *A Theology of Human Hope* (St. Meinrad, Ind.: Abbey Press, 1972), p. 71.
2. Gustavo Gutiérrez, *A Theology of Liberation* (Maryknoll, N.Y.: Orbis Books, 1972), p. 12.
3. Quoted in Donella H. Meadows et al., *The Limits to Growth* (New York: Universe Books, 1972), p. 17.
4. Ibid., p. 44.
5. See my article, "The Omrides of Jezreel," *Vetus Testamentum* 9 (1959): 366-78. See also O. H. Steck, *Überlieferung und Zeitgeschichte in den Elia-Erzählungen* (Neukirchen-Vluyn: 1968), p. 57, note 4.

Chapter Two: The Altars
1. This is not translation but paraphrase. The reading I prefer of the four Hebrew words is: So that this people may know "that you turned their heart backward"; that is, that you, Yahweh, are responsible, not Baal, for the backward heart. The alternate literal reading of the Hebrew is in any case implicit; that is, "that it is you who brings them back" (to their authentic alliegiance). The *sense* is not ambiguous. It is as Rashi put it (Rabbi Solomon bar Isaac, that magnificent rabbinic scholar of the eleventh century), "Thou gavest them place to depart from thee, and in thy hand it is to establish their heart toward thee." See further James A. Montgomery, *The Book of Kings* in *The International Critical Commentary*, ed. Henry Snyder Gehman (New York: Charles Scribner's Sons, 1951), p. 305.

2. One cannot help wondering whether "Elijah" may not have been an assumed name, a name given to the prophet subsequent to the event underlying the present narrative (whatever its factual proportions). The name means "My God is Yahweh," or even simply "God is Yahweh."

3. "For [this] ugly sequel, if authentic, the history of religion and politics down to our own day is sad apology" (Montgomery, *The Book of Kings*, p. 306). It appears to me to be in any case gratuitous to read, as Gunkel does (in an argument against the historicity of the event), "dass Elias die 450 Propheten Baals *mit eigener Hand* geschlachtet habe" (Hermann Gunkel, *Elias, Jahwe und Baal* [Tübingen: 1906], p. 36). The narrative does not here name the number, and it is improbable that all the prophets of Baal in the land were present at the Carmel assembly. The number 450 may not anywhere be reliable, and surely the statement that Elijah executed the Baal prophets does not require or warrant the reading "with his own hand."

4. This is, literally, the familiar biblical phrase "girded up his loins." The New English Bible puts it nicely: "he tucked up his robe."

5. Charles Y. Glock et al., *Wayward Shepherds* (New York: Harper & Row, 1971), pp. 95 and 121f.

6. Gutiérrez, *A Theology of Liberation*, pp. 26-27.

7. Ibid., p. 88.

8. Gunkel, *Elias, Jahwe und Baal*, p. 48.

9. I have borrowed this phrase in this context from Montgomery: "The clash of words between (Ahab) and the undaunted man of God is classical. The epithet, *Troubler of Israel*, is flung back in the king's teeth" (*The Book of Kings*, p. 299).

10. In an address prepared for delivery at Harvard University, June 13, 1974, on the occasion of his receiving an honorary doctorate in recognition of his defense of human rights. The address appeared in *Christianity and Crisis*, August 1974, p. 176.

11. There is dispute over the antiquity and priority of the two altars on Carmel, and in particular concerning the status of the Yahweh altar. But the symbolism of the two altars is not in question.

12. Gerhard von Rad, *Old Testament Theology,* vol. II, trans. D. M. G. Stalker (New York: Harper & Row, 1965), p. 17. Von Rad further comments here on why the people do not answer Elijah. Their silence "argues lack of understanding of the question rather than any feeling of guilt (v. 21). Elijah had to make a Herculean effort before he succeeded in forcing them to make a decision for which no one saw the need."

13. James Cone tells us that in the black community this is known as "shuffling." *A Black Theology of Liberation* (Philadelphia: Lippincott, 1970), p. 122.

14. Montgomery, *The Book of Kings,* p. 301.

15. J. Skinner, *Kings* in *The Century Bible* (Edinburgh: Oxford University Press, 1904), p. 231.

16. Rosemary Radford Ruether, *Liberation Theology* (New York: Paulist-Newman, 1972), p. 176.

17. Montgomery, *The Book of Kings,* p. 302.

18. Ibid., p. 306.

Chapter Three: The Cave

1. See von Rad, *Old Testament Theology,* p. 19.

2. The term is uncommon, appearing only seven times in the Old Testament.

3. Of all these, and of all that these may represent, sex in love surely has the best claim. Rosemary Ruether, in an essay on Judaism and Christianity, tells us that "far from despising sexuality, the rabbis even declared that, since the destruction of the temple, the presence of God existed in two places: in the rabbinic houses of study, and when a man lies beside his wife." Ruether, *Liberation Theology,* p. 70.

4. *Webster's Third New International Dictionary* (Springfield: G & C Merriam Company, 1965), italics mine.

5. Montgomery, *The Book of Kings,* pp. 314-15.

6. J. Skinner, *Isaiah* in *The International Critical Commentary* (New York: Charles Scribner's Sons, 1951), p. 205.

7. *The Continuing Quest,* ed. James B. Hofrenning (Minneapolis: Augsburg, 1970), p. 38.

8. Paulo Freire, *Pedagogy of the Oppressed,* trans. Myra Bergman Ramos (New York: Herder & Herder, 1970), p. 76.

9. Ibid., p. 142.
10. Ruether, *Liberation Theology*, p. 33.
11. Gutiérrez, *A Theology of Liberation*, pp. 71 and 76.
12. Dom Helder Camara, in *Christianity and Crisis*, August 1974, p. 176.
13. Freire, *Pedagogy of the Oppressed*, p. 24.
14. Rainer Maria Rilke, *Letters to a Young Poet*, trans. M. D. Herter Norton (New York: W. W. Norton, 1954, 1962), p. 67.
15. Ibid., p. 69.
16. Gary MacEoin, *Revolution Next Door* (New York: Holt, Rinehart & Winston, 1971), p. 129.

Chapter Four: The Inheritance

1. Rilke, *Letters to a Young Poet*, p. 23.
2. Ibid., p. 72.
3. *Guideposts*, August 1974, p. 19.
4. *Harvard Magazine*, vol. 76, no. 11 (July-August 1974), p. 63.
5. *Christianity and Crisis*, August 1974, pp. 175-77. Richard J. Barnet and Ronald Müller give specific content to Dom Helder Camara's words: "Global companies have used their great levels of power—finance capital, technology, organizational skills, and mass communications—to create a Global Shopping Center in which the hungry of the world are invited to buy expensive snacks and a Global Factory in which there are fewer and fewer jobs. The World Manager's vision of One World turns out in fact to be two distinct worlds—one featuring rising affluence for a small transitional middle class, and the other escalating misery for the great bulk of the human family. The dictates of profits and the dictates of survival are in clear conflict." Richard J. Barnet and Ronald Müller, *Global Reach: The Power of the Multinational Corporations* (New York: Simon and Schuster, 1974), p. 184.
6. *Christianity and Crisis*, August 1974, p. 177.
7. My own reasons for seeing all the action as occurring in Jezreel are discussed in "The Omrides of Jezreel" in *Vetus Testamentum*, 9 (1959): 366-78.
8. Quoted in *A Track to the Water's Edge: The Olive Schreiner Reader*, ed. Howard Thurman (New York: Harper & Row, 1973), p. xxvii, from her *Thoughts on South Africa*, p. 345.

9. Johannes Pedersen, *Israel: Its Life and Culture,* vol. I-II (London: Oxford University Press, 1940), p. 81.
10. Ibid., pp. 82-83. Nevertheless, as H. Seebass has remarked in "Der Fall Naboth in 1 Reg. XXI," *Vetus Testamentum,* 24 (1974): 476-77, there had to be conditions under which Naboth's vineyard was saleable or exchangeable, since otherwise Ahab's straightforward request and his response of bitter disappointment make no sense.
11. *Die Bücher der Könige,* 2 vols. (Münster: 1911); quoted in Montgomery, *The Book of Kings,* p. 331.
12. For this insight I am grateful to Seebass ("Der Fall Naboth in 1 Reg. XXI," p. 481): "Von einem Urteil nirgendwo die Rede ist. Dagegen hatte Isebel die Genugtuung, dass Naboth (scheinbar zu Recht) im Namen der Religion gesteinigt wurde, wie er im *Namen der Religion* den Könige zurückgewiesen hatte."
13. Georg Fohrer, *Elia,* vol. 53 in *Abhandlungen zur Theologie des Alten and Neuen Testaments* (Zürich, 2d ed., 1968), p. 28.